RESTful Java Web Services Security

Secure your RESTful applications against common vulnerabilities

René Enríquez

Andrés Salazar C.

BIRMINGHAM - MUMBAI

RESTful Java Web Services Security

First published: July 2014

Production reference: 1180714

Published by Packt Publishing Ltd.
Livery Place
35 Livery Street
Birmingham B3 2PB, UK.

ISBN 978-1-78398-010-9

www.packtpub.com

Cover image by Vivek Thangaswamy (vivekthangaswamy@yahoo.com)

Credits

Authors

René Enríquez

Andrés Salazar C.

Reviewers

Erik Azar

Ismail Marmoush

Debasis Roy

Acquisition Editor

Vinay Argekar

Content Development Editor

Adrian Raposo

Technical Editor

Shruti Rawool

Copy Editor

Sayanee Mukherjee

Project Coordinators

Melita Lobo

Harshal Ved

Proofreaders

Simran Bhogal

Paul Hindle

Indexers

Hemangini Bari

Rekha Nair

Graphics

Abhinash Sahu

Production Coordinator

Arvindkumar Gupta

Cover Work

Arvindkumar Gupta

About the Authors

René Enríquez is currently a software architect for a multinational company headquartered in India. He has previously worked on many projects related to security implementation using frameworks such as JAAS and Spring Security to integrate many platforms based on the Web, BPM, CMS, and web services for government and private sector companies. He is a technology and innovation enthusiast, and he is currently working with several programming languages. He has achieved the following certifications:

- Oracle Certified Professional, Java SE 6 Programmer
- Microsoft Technology Associate
- Cisco Network Operating Systems

Over the past few years, he has worked as a software consultant on various projects for private and government companies and as an instructor of courses to build enterprise and mobile applications. He is also an evangelist of best practices for application development and integration.

Andrés Salazar C. is currently working at one of the most prestigious government companies in Ecuador, performing tasks related to software development and security implementation based on JAAS and digital signatures for secure applications. He also has extensive knowledge of OAuth implementation on web projects. He is a technology and Agile enthusiast, and he has worked on several projects using the JEE technology and TDD. He has achieved the following certifications:

- Oracle Certified Professional, Java SE 6 Programmer
- Certified Scrum Developer

About the Reviewers

Erik Azar is a professional software developer with over 20 years of experience in the areas of system administration, network engineering and security, development, and architecture. Having worked in diverse positions in companies ranging from start-ups to Fortune 500 companies, he currently works as a REST API architect for Availity, LLC in Jacksonville, FL. He is a dedicated Linux hobbyist who enjoys kernel hacking while experimenting with Raspberry Pi and BeagleBone Black boards. In his spare time, he works on solutions using embedded microprocessor platforms, Bluetooth 4.0, and connects to the cloud using RESTful APIs.

Ismail Marmoush is a Java and Machine Learning Certified Expert. He has published the open source projects RESTful Boilerplates for IAAS and PAAS (GAE), an artificial neural network framework, and crawlers/dataminers and some language code examples. You can find more about him, his work, and his tutorials on his personal blog (`http://marmoush.com`).

Thanks to my family and the Packt Publishing team.

Debasis Roy is working as the Team Lead / Scrum Master of the sports team for Vizrt Bangladesh based at Dhaka. He has 7 years of professional working experience as a software engineer in Java/C++-relevant technologies.

He has been working at Vizrt for the past 5 years. He started his journey here with a product called the Online Suite, also known as Escenic Content Engine/Studio, and he is now continuing with products related to Viz Sports. Vizrt provides real-time 3D graphics, studio automation, sports analysis, and asset management tools for the broadcast industry—interactive and virtual solutions, animations, maps, weather forecasts, video editing, and compositing tools.

Previously, he worked at SDSL/AfriGIS for 2 years, where he was involved mainly in the projects, Marbil and Grid. AfriGIS is a technology innovation company that creates geographic information and communication solutions.

www.PacktPub.com

Support files, eBooks, discount offers, and more

You might want to visit www.PacktPub.com for support files and downloads related to your book.

Did you know that Packt offers eBook versions of every book published, with PDF and ePub files available? You can upgrade to the eBook version at www.PacktPub.com and as a print book customer, you are entitled to a discount on the eBook copy. Get in touch with us at service@packtpub.com for more details.

At www.PacktPub.com, you can also read a collection of free technical articles, sign up for a range of free newsletters and receive exclusive discounts and offers on Packt books and eBooks.

http://PacktLib.PacktPub.com

Do you need instant solutions to your IT questions? PacktLib is Packt's online digital book library. Here, you can access, read and search across Packt's entire library of books.

Why subscribe?

- Fully searchable across every book published by Packt
- Copy and paste, print and bookmark content
- On demand and accessible via web browser

Free access for Packt account holders

If you have an account with Packt at www.PacktPub.com, you can use this to access PacktLib today and view nine entirely free books. Simply use your login credentials for immediate access.

Table of Contents

Preface

The inherent advantages of the use of web services in computer systems development are the same that create the need for security management over them. Today, we can say that no company is able to work in complete isolation, without the need to interact with others and share and consume information. Furthermore, this is the most important asset of any company. For this reason, these requirements are also common between lines of code. This book presents real scenarios with applicable solutions, leading you by the hand all the way, so you can easily learn solutions and implementations that will resolve the most common needs that can arise.

RESTful web services offer several advantages over those based on SOAP. For example, when handling data types, depending on the programming language or the libraries you use to create them, you can find inconsistencies when using empty values ("") instead of NULL. Also, you may find difficulties in mapping complex objects and compatibility issues in file transferring when using different versions of libraries to create/consume the web service. In certain situations, even when consuming a web service created in Java from a .NET application, it ends up creating a service implemented in Java in the middle of both. This does not occur in RESTful web services, since in this case, the functionality is exposed through HTTP method invocations.

In order to protect information, the world of securities has many features that help to achieve this. For example, understanding how some issues such as authentication and authorization assist in the implementation of any selected mechanism, where the main objective is to make our applications safer and secure, is essential. The selection of each of the different ways to secure applications goes along with the problem you want to resolve; for this, we show usage scenarios for each of them.

Many times, we have seen large organizations spend time and effort in creating their own implementations to handle securities rather than using the standard that has already resolved what we need. Through the knowledge that we want to share with you, we hope to avoid this process of reinventing the wheel.

What this book covers

Chapter 1, Setting Up the Environment, helps us create our first functional application, something very similar to a *Hello World* example, but with some more functionality and very close to the real world. The main aim of this chapter is to familiarize ourselves with the tools we are going to use.

Chapter 2, The Importance of Securing Web Services, goes through all possible models of authentication in the Java platform. For your better understanding, we will go step by step and dive deep into how we can leverage each available authentication model. We will show you how the information is exposed and how it can be intercepted by third parties, and we will play with Wireshark, which is a very good tool to explain it.

Finally, in this chapter, we will review the differences between authentication and authorization. Both concepts are very important and definitely impossible to put aside in the context of securities terms.

Chapter 3, Security Management with RESTEasy, shows how RESTEasy offers mechanisms to handle security, starting from a fairly basic model (coarse-grained) to a more elaborate one (fine-grained) in which you can perform more exhaustive controls, including managing not only configuration files, but also programmatical files.

Chapter 4, RESTEasy Skeleton Key, helps us study the OAuth implementation along with the token bearer implementation and Single Sign-On. All of them are used in order to limit the way the resources are shared. As always, you will get hands-on with code and real examples. We want to show you how sharing resources and information between applications through these technologies has turned into one of the most useful and powerful techniques by allowing clients or users to use their credentials only once to access several services, limiting the access to third-party applications to your information or data, and implementing access control through the token bearer. You will learn to apply these technologies and concepts in order to build secure and flexible applications.

Chapter 5, Digital Signatures and Encryption of Messages, helps us understand the benefits of digital signatures using a simple example; you'll notice how the message's receiver can validate the identity of the sender. In addition, we will simulate when an external agent modifies data in transit and see how digital signatures can help us to detect it, in order to avoid working with corrupted data.

Finally, we will explain SMIME for body encryption and how it works, with an example that encrypts requests and responses for your better understanding.

What you need for this book

In order to implement and test all the examples in this book, we will use many free tools, such as the following:

- Eclipse IDE (or any other Java IDE)
- JBoss AS 7
- Maven
- Wireshark
- SoapUI

Who this book is for

This book is intended for developers, software analysts, architects, or people who work with software development and RESTful web services. This book requires some previous knowledge of object-oriented programming concepts in Java or any other language.

No previous knowledge on security models is required because we explain the theory and apply it on practical examples in this book.

Conventions

In this book, you will find a number of styles of text that distinguish between different kinds of information. Here are some examples of these styles, and an explanation of their meaning.

Code words in text, database table names, folder names, filenames, file extensions, pathnames, dummy URLs, user input, and Twitter handles are shown as follows: "We are going to modify the web.xml file."

A block of code is set as follows:

```
private boolean isUserAllowed(final String username, final String
password, final Set<String> rolesSet) {
    boolean isAllowed = false;
    if (rolesSet.contains(ADMIN)) {
      isAllowed = true;
    }
    return isAllowed;
  }
}
```

When we wish to draw your attention to a particular part of a code block, the relevant lines or items are set in bold:

```
final List<String> authorizationList = headersMap.get(AUTHORIZATION_
PROPERTY);
```

Any command-line input or output is written as follows:

```
mvn clean install
```

New terms and **important** words are shown in bold. Words that you see on the screen, in menus or dialog boxes for example, appear in the text like this: "From the pop-up window, select the **SSL Settings** tab."

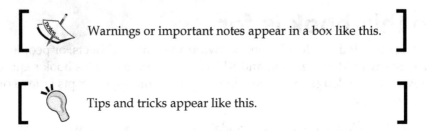

Warnings or important notes appear in a box like this.

Tips and tricks appear like this.

Reader feedback

Feedback as suggestions or comments from our readers is always welcome. Let us know what you think about this book—what you liked or may have disliked. Reader feedback is important for us to develop titles that you really get the most out of and also to improve the way we transmit knowledge.

To send us general feedback, simply send an e-mail to feedback@packtpub.com, and mention the book title via the subject of your message.

If there is a topic that you have expertise in and you are interested in either writing or contributing to a book, see our author guide on www.packtpub.com/authors.

Customer support

Now that you are the proud owner of a Packt book, we have a number of things to help you to get the most from your purchase.

Downloading the example code

You can download the example code files for all Packt books you have purchased from your account at http://www.packtpub.com. If you purchased this book elsewhere, you can visit http://www.packtpub.com/support and register to have the files e-mailed directly to you. Also, we highly suggest obtaining the source code from GitHub available at https://github.com/restful-java-web-services-security.

Errata

Although we have taken every care to ensure the accuracy of our content, mistakes do happen. If you find a mistake in one of our books — maybe a mistake in the text or the code — we would be grateful if you would report this to us. By doing so, you can save other readers from frustration and help us improve subsequent versions of this book. If you find any errata, please report them by visiting http://www.packtpub.com/submit-errata, selecting your book, clicking on the **errata submission form** link, and entering the details of your errata. Once your errata are verified, your submission will be accepted and the errata will be uploaded on our website, or added to any list of existing errata, under the Errata section of that title. Any existing errata can be viewed by selecting your title from http://www.packtpub.com/support.

Piracy

Piracy of copyright material on the Internet is an ongoing problem across all media. At Packt, we take the protection of our copyright and licenses very seriously. If you come across any illegal copies of our works, in any form, on the Internet, please provide us with the location address or website name immediately so that we can pursue a remedy.

Please contact us at copyright@packtpub.com with a link to the suspected pirated material.

We appreciate your help in protecting our authors, and our ability to bring you valuable content.

Questions

You can contact us at questions@packtpub.com if you are having a problem with any aspect of the book, and we will do our best to address it.

Setting Up the Environment

1

We extend you a very warm welcome to the first chapter of our journey. Let's give you an idea of what you will achieve here. After reading this chapter, you will have the basic and stimulating knowledge you need to set up a development environment to work with RESTful web services. Then, you will familiarize yourself with the development of a very basic project related to it. In addition, by the end, you will have a very clear idea of how to create applications using RESTful web services and how you can achieve this. This chapter will give you the information you need to work with web services of this kind in a very easy and comprehensive way.

In this chapter, we will cover the following topics:

- Installing the development environment
- Creating our first RESTful web services application
- Testing the RESTful web service

Downloading tools

First, we must obtain our work tools so that we get our hands into code. Tools specified here are used around the world, but you are free to choose your tools. Remember, "Tools do not make the artist". It doesn't matter if you use Windows, MAC OS X, or Linux; tools are available for every OS.

Let's explain briefly what each tool is for. We will develop the examples using Eclipse as our IDE, JBoss AS 7.1.1.Final as our application server, Maven to automatize the build process, and SoapUI as a tool to test the functionality of web services that we will create. In addition, we suggest that you should install the latest version of JDK, which is JDK 1.7.x. For help, we have obtained and included some links that you need to use to get the software to implement the first example. Each link gives you more information about each tool, which can be profitable as you learn something about each one if you don't know about them already.

Downloading links

The following tools have to be downloaded:

- Eclipse IDE for Java EE Developers 4.3 (`http://www.eclipse.org/downloads/`)

- JBoss AS 7.1.1 Final (`http://www.jboss.org/jbossas/downloads/`)

- Apache Maven 3.1.1 or higher (`http://maven.apache.org/download.cgi`)

- SoapUI 4.6 or higher (`http://www.soapui.org/`)

- JDK 1.7.x (`http://www.oracle.com/technetwork/java/javase/downloads/jdk7-downloads-1880260.html`)

Creating the base project

In order to make the process of building our sample project easier, we will use Maven. This wonderful software will create a base project at the blink of an eye, and our project can be easily compiled and packaged without depending on a specific IDE.

Maven uses archetypes for a specific kind of project. The archetypes are project templates that have been previously created; they allow us to create all kinds of applications from Java desktop applications to multimodule projects, where the EAR can contain several artifacts such as JAR and WAR. Its main objective is to get users up and running as quickly as possible by providing a sample project that demonstrates many of the features of Maven. If you want to learn more about Maven, you can find more information by visiting `http://maven.apache.org/`.

However, the information we described here is enough to keep moving on. We will use an archetype in order to create a basic project; if we want to be more specific, we will use an archetype to create a web application with Java. To do this, we will type the following command line in a terminal:

```
mvn archetype:generate
```

When we execute this command line in a terminal, we will obtain all available archetypes in Maven's repository. So, let's look for the archetype we need in order to create our web application; its name is `webapp-javaee6`, and it belongs to the group `org.codehaus.mojo.archetypes`. Also, we can search through it using a number that represents its ID; this number is `557`, as shown in the following screenshot. We recommend that you search by the name as the numbers are likely to change because some other archetypes may be added later:

```
● ○ ○                                                              W
551: remote -> org.codehaus.mojo.archetypes:netbeans-platform-app-archetype
NBM project.)
552: remote -> org.codehaus.mojo.archetypes:osgi-archetype (Archetype for de
553: remote -> org.codehaus.mojo.archetypes:pom-root (Root project archetype
554: remote -> org.codehaus.mojo.archetypes:sample-javafx (Sample archetype
555: remote -> org.codehaus.mojo.archetypes:webapp-j2ee13 (-)
556: remote -> org.codehaus.mojo.archetypes:webapp-j2ee14 (-)
557: remote -> org.codehaus.mojo.archetypes:webapp-javaee6 (-)
558: remote -> org.codehaus.mojo.archetypes:webapp-javaee7 (Archetype for a
559: remote -> org.codehaus.mojo.archetypes:webapp-jee5 (-)
```

Several questions will appear; we must provide the respective information for each question. Maven will use this information to create the archetype we selected before, as shown in the following screenshot:

```
Choose org.codehaus.mojo.archetypes:webapp-javaee6 version:
1: 1.0
2: 1.0.1
3: 1.0.2
4: 1.1
5: 1.2
6: 1.3
7: 1.4
8: 1.5
Choose a number: 8: 8
Define value for property 'groupId': : com.packtpub
Define value for property 'artifactId': : resteasy-examples
Define value for property 'version':  1.0-SNAPSHOT: :
Define value for property 'package':  com.packtpub: :
Confirm properties configuration:
groupId: com.packtpub
artifactId: resteasy-examples
version: 1.0-SNAPSHOT
package: com.packtpub
```

As you have probably noticed, each question asks you to define a property, and each property is explained as follows:

- `groupId`: This property represents the company's domain reversed order; this way we can recognize which company is the code's owner
- `artifactId`: This property represents the project's name
- `version`: This property represents the project's version
- `package`: This property represents the base package's name where classes are going to be added

Class names and package names together shape the class's full name. This full name allows the class names to be identified in a unique way. Sometimes, when there are several classes with the same name, the package name helps to identify which library it belongs to.

The next step is to put the project into Eclipse's workspace; to do this, we must import our project into Eclipse by navigating through **File | Import | Maven | Existing Maven Projects**.

We should see the project in the IDE, as shown in the following screenshot:

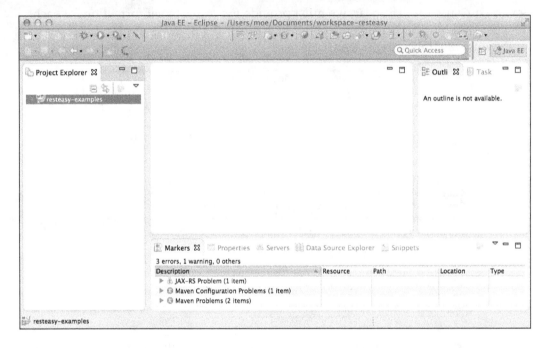

Before moving on, let's fix the problems that have occurred in the file pom.xml.

The error shown in the following code is related to a bug that comes from Eclipse and Maven integration. In order to fix this, we have to add the <pluginManagement> tag after the <build> tag.

The pom.xml file should look like the following:

```
<project xmlns="http://maven.apache.org/POM/4.0.0" xmlns:xsi="http://
www.w3.org/2001/XMLSchema-instance"
  xsi:schemaLocation="http://maven.apache.org/POM/4.0.0 http://maven.
apache.org/xsd/maven-4.0.0.xsd">
  <modelVersion>4.0.0</modelVersion>

  <groupId>com.packtpub</groupId>
  <artifactId>resteasy-examples</artifactId>
  <version>1.0-SNAPSHOT</version>
  <packaging>war</packaging>

  .  .  .

  <build>
    <pluginManagement>
      <plugins>
        <plugin>
          .  .  .
        </plugin>
      </plugins>
    </pluginManagement>
  </build>

</project>
```

Downloading the sample code

You can download the sample code files for all Packt books you have purchased from your account at http://www.packtpub.com. If you purchased this book elsewhere, you can visit http://www.packtpub.com/support and register to have the files e-mailed directly to you. Also, we highly suggest obtaining the source code from GitHub available at https://github.com/restful-java-web-services-security.

This will fix the error, and now we only need to update Maven's configuration in the project, as shown in the following screenshot:

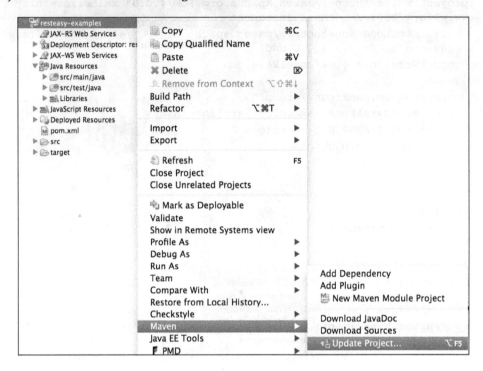

After refreshing the project, the errors should go away because when we update Maven's configuration we are actually updating our project's dependencies, such as missing libraries. Through this, we will include them in our project and errors will disappear.

Inside the `src/main/webapp` path, let's create the `WEB-INF` folder.

Now, inside the `WEB-INF` folder, we will create a new file named `web.xml` with the following content:

```xml
<?xml version="1.0" encoding="UTF-8"?>
<web-app version="3.0" xmlns="http://java.sun.com/xml/ns/javaee"
  xmlns:xsi="http://www.w3.org/2001/XMLSchema-instance"
  xsi:schemaLocation="http://java.sun.com/xml/ns/javaee
  http://java.sun.com/xml/ns/javaee/web-app_3_0.xsd">
</web-app>
```

This file is very useful when you are securing your applications; this time, we will create it without any configuration. For now, the `/WEB-INF` folder and the `web.xml` file only define the structure of the web application.

First functional example

Now that we have our development environment all set up, it is time to get your hands dirty and write the first RESTful web service. As we are using JBoss, let's use the RESTEasy implementation for JAX-RS. We will develop a very simple example; let's imagine you want to implement a service to save and search for people's information.

First, we create a simple `Person` domain class that uses JAXB annotations. JAXB marshals/unmarshals objects between XML and Java. For this example, we'll store these instances in an in-memory cache instead of a database. In JEE, this typically represents a table in a relational database, and each entity instance corresponds to a row in that table, as presented in the following code:

```
package com.packtpub.resteasy.entities;

import javax.xml.bind.annotation.XmlAccessType;
import javax.xml.bind.annotation.XmlAccessorType;
import javax.xml.bind.annotation.XmlAttribute;
import javax.xml.bind.annotation.XmlElement;
import javax.xml.bind.annotation.XmlRootElement;

@XmlRootElement(name = "person")
@XmlAccessorType(XmlAccessType.FIELD)
public class Person {

  @XmlAttribute
  protected int id;

  @XmlElement
  protected String name;

  @XmlElement
  protected String lastname;

  public int getId() {
    return id;
  }

  public void setId(int id) {
    this.id = id;
  }

  public String getName() {
```

```
        return name;
    }

    public void setName(String name) {
        this.name = name;
    }

    public String getLastname() {
        return lastname;
    }

    public void setLastname(String lastname) {
        this.lastname = lastname;
    }


}
```

Next, we create a new class called `PersonService` in the `com.packtpub.resteasy.services` package. This class will have two methods; one to register a new person and another to search for people by ID. This class will store people using an in-memory map cache.

The service will have the following implementation:

```
package com.packtpub.resteasy.services;

import java.net.URI;
import java.util.HashMap;
import java.util.Map;

import javax.ws.rs.Consumes;
import javax.ws.rs.GET;
import javax.ws.rs.POST;
import javax.ws.rs.Path;
import javax.ws.rs.PathParam;
import javax.ws.rs.Produces;
import javax.ws.rs.WebApplicationException;
import javax.ws.rs.core.Response;

import com.packtpub.resteasy.entities.Person;

@Path("/person")
public class PersonService {
    private Map<Integer, Person> dataInMemory;
    public PersonService() {
```

```
      dataInMemory = new HashMap<Integer, Person>();
  }

  @POST
  @Consumes("application/xml")
  public Response savePerson(Person person) {
    int id = dataInMemory.size() + 1;
    person.setId(id);
    dataInMemory.put(id, person);
    return Response.created(URI.create("/person/" + id)).build();
  }

  @GET
  @Path("{id}")
  @Produces("application/xml")
  public Person findById(@PathParam("id") int id) {
    Person person = dataInMemory.get(id);
    if (person == null) {
      throw new WebApplicationException(Response.Status.NOT_FOUND);
    }
    return person;
  }
}
```

The @Path annotation defines the path in the URL that will be available on the functionalities that have been written within this class. The method annotated with @Post indicates that it should make a HTTP POST request. Furthermore, it is annotated with @Consumes and uses the application/xml value; this means that the POST request will be performed with a string in XML format, containing the information of the person to be saved. On the other hand, to find a person from its ID, you must make an HTTP GET request. The URL must indicate the ID the same way as indicated by the @Path annotation on the method. The @Produces annotation indicates that we will get the response in XML format. Finally, notice that the parameter ID, as indicated in the @Path annotation, is used as an argument of the method using the @PathParam annotation.

Finally, we write a class that will extend the Application class and set the service we just created as a singleton. So, the information won't get lost in every request, and we will keep it in memory as follows:

```
package com.packtpub.resteasy.services;

import java.util.HashSet;
```

```
import java.util.Set;

import javax.ws.rs.ApplicationPath;
import javax.ws.rs.core.Application;

@ApplicationPath("/services")
public class MyRestEasyApplication extends Application {

  private Set<Object> services;

  public MyRestEasyApplication() {
    services = new HashSet<Object>();
    services.add(new PersonService());
  }

  @Override
  public Set<Object> getSingletons() {
    return services;
  }
}
```

Note that as we have mapped our entity using JAXB, our methods consume and produce information in the XML format.

In order to deploy our application in JBoss, we should add a dependency in the pom. xml file. This dependency must reference to the JBoss plugin. We have to change the generated artifact name in pom.xml. The default value for this is the artifactId file, followed by the version; for example, resteasy-examples-1.0-snapshot.war. We will set it, so we will use just the artifactId file; in this case, resteasy-examples. war. All of these configurations must be included, modified, and implemented in pom.xml, as shown in the following piece of XML code:

```
<build>
  <finalName>${artifactId}</finalName>
  <pluginManagement>
    <plugins>
      <plugin>
        <groupId>org.jboss.as.plugins</groupId>
        <artifactId>jboss-as-maven-plugin</artifactId>
        <version>7.5.Final</version>
        <configuration>
          <jbossHome>/pathtojboss/jboss-as-
            7.1.1.Final</jbossHome>
        </configuration>
      </plugin>
```

```
        . . .
      </plugin>
    </plugins>
  </pluginManagement>
</build>
```

You should change the value of the `jbossHome` property for the path of your JBoss installation. After this, we will use the command terminal; head to the project's directory, and type `mvn jboss-as:run`. If you make any change on the code after the command has been executed, then you should use the following command in order to see the changes:

`mvn jboss-as:redeploy`

Run and redeploy are the goals of this plugin. If you want to know more goals about this plugin, you can visit `https://docs.jboss.org/jbossas/7/plugins/maven/latest/`). This will compile all project classes again; it will then be packaged in order to create the `.war` file. At the end, the modifications will be deployed on the server. If everything is okay, we should see a message in the terminal saying that the deployment has been done successfully, as shown in the following screenshot:

```
⊖ ○ ○                    bin — java — 96×14
        java                        bash
00:39:15,164 INFO  [org.jboss.as.repository] (management-handler-thread - 1) JBAS014900: Content
 added at location /Users/moe/Documents/Java/jboss-as-7.1.1.Final/standalone/data/content/fa/939
3869a551e881973c3f6b2109ee1c5decb01/content
00:39:15,191 INFO  [org.jboss.as.server.deployment] (MSC service thread 1-5) JBAS015877: Stopped
 deployment resteasy-examples.war in 22ms
00:39:15,193 INFO  [org.jboss.as.server.deployment] (MSC service thread 1-7) JBAS015876: Startin
g deployment of "resteasy-examples.war"
00:39:15,230 INFO  [org.jboss.web] (MSC service thread 1-7) JBAS018210: Registering web context:
 /resteasy-examples
00:39:15,267 INFO  [org.jboss.as.server] (management-handler-thread - 1) JBAS018562: Redeployed
"resteasy-examples.war"
00:39:15,267 INFO  [org.jboss.as.server] (management-handler-thread - 1) JBAS018565: Replaced de
ployment "resteasy-examples.war" with deployment "resteasy-examples.war"
```

The source code of this chapter is available on GitHub at the following location:

`https://github.com/restful-java-web-services-security/source-code/tree/master/chapter01`

Testing the example web service

At this moment, we will test the functionality we just created. We will use SoapUI as our test tool; make sure you use the latest version, or at least the version equal to or greater than 4.6.x because this version offers more features to test the RESTful Web services. Let's start by performing the following steps:

1. From the main menu, let's create a new REST project by navigating to **File | New REST Project**, as shown in the following screenshot:

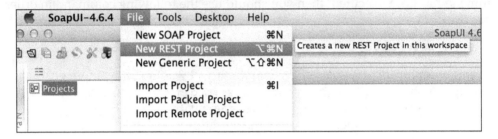

2. Set the URI of our service, as follows:

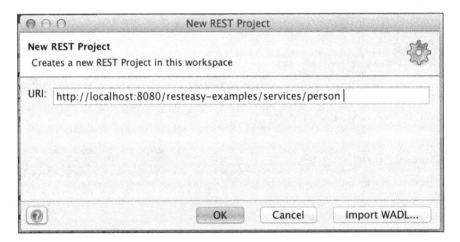

3. After this, let's create a new person using the POST method from workspace. In the field **Media Type**, select **application/xml** and perform a request with a string that contains the XML with the information, as shown in the following text:

```
<person><name>Rene</name><lastname>Enriquez</lastname></person>
```

4. When we click on the **Play** button, we should obtain an answer where it shows the created resource URI (hyperlink "`http://localhost:8080/resteasy-examples/services/person/1`"), as shown in the following screenshot:

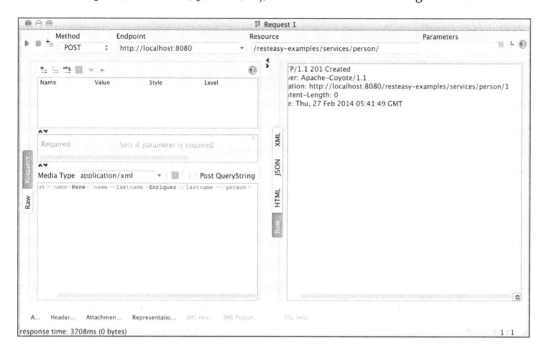

5. If we change the URI from the **Resource** textbox in SoapUI and use the GET method, it will show us the data we just entered, as shown in the following screenshot:

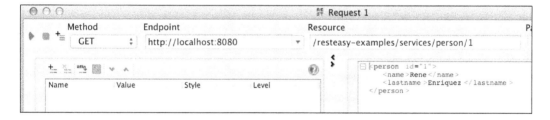

Congratulations! We have developed our first functional RESTful web service with two features. The first is to keep people's information in memory, and the second is to retrieve people's information through an ID.

 If you restart JBoss or deploy the application again, all data will be lost. Before searching for people's information, you must first save the data.

Summary

In this chapter, we created our first functional application—something like a *hello world* example but with a bit more functionality close to the real world.

The essential part we covered in this chapter is to familiarize ourselves with the tools we will use. In later chapters, we will assume that these concepts are already clear. For example, we will move forward step-by-step when using SoapUI as this is a tool that will facilitate the task of testing the functionality that we will be developing. This way, we will avoid the task of writing code for web service clients.

Now we are ready to review the next chapter, which contains some security models that Java provides. We will understand each one of them and learn how to implement them.

2
The Importance of Securing Web Services

Look at you; you have made it to Chapter 2; congratulations! This chapter is quite important because it is related to a concept that is implicit in software, which is **security**. This is very important because software is used by companies and people like us. Sometimes, we share very important and confidential information through software, and that is why this topic becomes so important for everybody.

In this chapter, we will take you through the basic aspects related to the management of security in computer systems.

We will explore and implement each of the different security mechanisms and scenarios in which they can be used.

Also, you'll learn how to use a protocol analyzer. This will allow us to demonstrate how an attack can be performed and determine the impact of this attack when it achieves its target, in this case, our information. Also, you will be able to imagine more options to implement security in web services.

As everything needs practice, you will go through a simple example of code to learn the differences between authentication and authorization. Get ready for an interesting and useful topic.

In this chapter, we will cover the following:

- Understanding the importance of security management
- Exploring and implementing the different available mechanisms of security
- Using a protocol analyzer to intercept requests
- Understanding the difference between authentication and authorization

The importance of security

The management of security is one of the main aspects to consider when designing applications.

No matter what, neither the functionality nor the information of organizations can be exposed to all users without any kind of restriction. Consider the case of a human resource management application that allows you to consult the wages of employees, for example: if the company manager needs to know the salary of one of their employees, it is not something of great importance. However, in the same context, imagine that one of the employees wants to know the salary of their colleagues; if access to this information is completely open, it can generate problems among employees with varied salaries.

An even more critical example can be the case where the bank XYZ increases a bank balance every time a customer or a third party makes a deposit into one of their accounts using an ATM. The IT manager envisions that this functionality could be common, and decides to implement it as a web service. Right now, this functionality is limited to bank users logged in to the application that uses this web service. Suppose that the visions of the future of the IT manager come true, and this functionality is now required from an ATM; raising this requirement quickly indicates that such functionality is implemented and can be used by invoking the web service. So far, there may be no security loopholes since ATMs are likely to have a security system that controls access, and thus operating system access to the functionality of the web service is also indirectly controlled.

Now, imagine that the company ABC wants a similar functionality to increase the balance in one of its employee's bank account by an x amount in recognition of some kind of contribution to the company. What happens to the functionality of the web service? Do you think you can again trust the application that handles its own security scheme to control access to its functionality? Even if we do trust this mechanism, what if the request is intercepted by a sniffer? Then, anyone who knows how to perform the request may increase the balance. These questions, when answered, throw in the response in quite a logical way. Exposed, these scenarios now sound quite logical so that whoever authenticates the user to have access to this functionality is the web service, and as such, should be entrusted with the management scheme security systems under all circumstances. It doesn't matter if invocations are from the organization itself or from an external institution; security control must be present in order to expose a sensitive functionality such as the one we just outlined.

When sharing existing information or functionality through web services, it is well known that we don't depend on programming languages, architectures, or system platforms to interact with. This gives us flexibility and saves us from having to rewrite the existing functionality. Going further, we should understand that these features have an impact on data confidentiality, as we are going to share information and/or functionality with entities or systems. This way, we can accomplish the business objectives and definitely prevent intruders from reading our information; or even worse, a third party not authorized has access to functionalities exposed by our services. Hence, access to them must be rigorously analyzed and our exposed services must be correctly ensured.

Security management options

Java provides some options for security management. Right now, we will explain some of them and demonstrate how to implement them. All authentication methods are practically based on credential delivery from the client to the server. There are several methods to perform this, which are:

- BASIC authentication
- DIGEST authentication
- CLIENT CERT authentication
- Using API keys

Security management in applications built with Java, including the ones with RESTful web services, always rely on JAAS.

Java Authentication and Authorization Service (JAAS) is a framework that is part of Java Platform Enterprise Edition. Hence, it is the default standard to handle an application's security in Java; it allows you to implement authorization, and it allows authentication controls over applications with the purpose of protecting resources that belong to the application. If you want to know more about JAAS, you can check out the following link:

```
http://docs.oracle.com/javase/7/docs/technotes/guides/security/jaas/
tutorials/GeneralAcnOnly.html
```

If you don't want to use JAAS, of course it is always possible to create our own implementation to handle securities, but it would be hard. So, why don't we save ourselves some time, effort, and peace by implementing this useful technology? It is recommended to use standard implementations whenever possible. In our development exercise, we will use JAAS for the first three methods of authentication.

Authorization and authentication

When you these terms, it is very easy to get confused, but they have different meanings when you have a security system approach. In order to clarify these terms, we will explain them in this section.

Authentication

In a nutshell, this term refers to *who you are*. It is the process to identify a user, usually through their *username* and *password*. When we use this concept, we are trying to ensure the identity of the user and we verify the identity the user claims to be. Also, it doesn't have anything to do with the access rights the user has.

Security research has specified a list of factors that should be verified in order to achieve positive authentication. This list contains three elements, where it is very common to use two of them, but preferably we should use all of them. These elements are the following:

- **Knowledge factors**: This element implies something the user **knows**, for example, a password, pass phrase, or personal identification number (PIN). Another example is challenge response, where the user must answer a question, software token, or phone serving as a software token.

- **Ownership factors**: This is something the user *has*, for example, a wrist band (in case of physical authentication), ID card, security token, or cell phone with a built-in hardware token.

- **Inherence factors**: This is something the user *is* or *does*, for example, fingerprint or retinal pattern, DNA sequence, signature, face, voice, unique bio-electric signals, or other biometric identifiers.

Authorization

In a few words, this term refers to *what you can do*. It is the process of giving a user permission to do or have something. When we talk about software, we have a system administrator that is in charge of defining the system which users are allowed to access and what the privileges of use are (such as access to which file directories, access period, amount of allocated storage space, and so forth).

Authorization is often seen as both the introductory setting up of permissions by a system administrator and the checking of the permission values that have already been set up when a user is getting access.

Access control

A very common use of authentication and authorization is access control. A computer system that is supposed to be used only by authorized users must attempt to detect and reject unauthorized users. Access is controlled by persisting on an authentication process to establish the user's identity with a certain level of confidence, also conferring privileges specified for that identity. Let's name some examples of access control involving authentication in different scenarios, such as the following:

- Calling for photo ID when a contractor first arrives at a house to do some work
- Implementing captcha as a way of verification that a user is a human being and not a computer program
- When using a **One Time Password** (**OTP**) obtained on telenetwork-enabled devices such as mobile phones as an authentication password/PIN
- A computer program that uses a blind credential in order to authenticate to another program
- When you enter a country with a passport
- When you log in to a computer
- When a service uses a confirmation e-mail to verify ownership of an e-mail address
- Using an Internet banking system
- When you withdraw cash from an ATM

Sometimes, the ease of access is adjusted against the strictness of access checks. For example, a small transaction usually doesn't require a signature of the authenticated person as proof of the transaction's authorization.

However, security experts argue that it is impossible to prove the user's identity with absolute certainty. It is only possible to apply a set of tests which, if passed, have been previously declared as a minimum to confirm the identity. The problem lies in how to determine which tests are enough; it depends on the company to determine this set.

Transport layer security

In this section, we highlight some of the main features of TLS:

- Its predecessor is **Secure Sockets Layer** (**SSL**)
- It is a cryptographic protocol

- It provides security communication over the Internet
- It authenticates the counterpart through X.509 certificates (asymmetric cryptography)
- It allows client-server applications to communicate over the network and prevents eavesdropping and tampering
- TLS is often implemented on top of the Transport layer protocols
- It encapsulates application-specific protocols such as HTTP, FTP, SMTP, NNTP, and XMPP
- The use of TLS should be delegated, especially when credentials, updates, deletions, and any kind of value transactions are performed
- The overhead of TLS is very low on modern hardware, with a little increase of latency, but this represents more safety for the end user

Basic authentication by providing user credentials

Possibly, basic authentication is one of the most used techniques in all types of applications. The user, before gaining functionality over the application, is requested to enter a username and password. Both are validated in order to verify whether the credentials are correct (they belong to an application user). We are 99 percent sure you have performed this technique at least once, maybe through a customized mechanism, or if you have used the JEE platform, probably through JAAS. This kind of control is known as **basic authentication**.

The main problem with this security implementation is that credentials are propagated in a plain way from the client to the server. This way, any sniffer could read the sent packages over the network. We will consider an example using a tool named Wireshark; it is a protocol analyzer that will show this problem. For installation, we can go to the link `http://www.wireshark.org/download.html`.

The installation is pretty basic (click on **Next** all the way). For this reason, we will not show screenshots of these steps.

Now, we are going to modify the project from *Chapter 1, Setting Up the Environment*, where the user tries to invoke any of the functions of the web service. The user will be requested to enter a username and password; once these are verified, the user will have access to the web service functionality.

In order to have a working example, let's start our application server JBoss AS 7; then, go to the `bin` directory and execute the file `add-user.bat` (the `.sh` file for UNIX users). Finally, we will create a new user as follows:

```
MacBook-Pro-de-Rene:bin moe$ ./add-user.sh

What type of user do you wish to add?
 a) Management User (mgmt-users.properties)
 b) Application User (application-users.properties)
(a): b

Enter the details of the new user to add.
Realm (ApplicationRealm) : ApplicationRealm
Username : username
Password :
Re-enter Password :
What roles do you want this user to belong to? (Please enter a comma separated list,
or leave blank for none) : admin
About to add user 'username' for realm 'ApplicationRealm'
Is this correct yes/no? yes
Added user 'username' to file '/Users/moe/Documents/Java/jboss-as-7.1.1.Final/standal
one/configuration/application-users.properties'
Added user 'username' to file '/Users/moe/Documents/Java/jboss-as-7.1.1.Final/domain/
configuration/application-users.properties'
Added user 'username' with roles admin to file '/Users/moe/Documents/Java/jboss-as-7.
1.1.Final/standalone/configuration/application-roles.properties'
Added user 'username' with roles admin to file '/Users/moe/Documents/Java/jboss-as-7.
1.1.Final/domain/configuration/application-roles.properties'
MacBook-Pro-de-Rene:bin moe$
```

The most important thing here is that you should select `Application User` in the first question and assign it an `admin` role. This will match with the information defined in the `web.xml` file, which will be explained later when we implement securities inside our application. As a result, we will have a new user in the `JBOSS_HOME/standalone/configuration/application - users. properties` file.

JBoss is already set with a default security domain called `other`; this domain uses the information stored in the file we mentioned earlier in order to authenticate. Right now, we will configure the application to use this security domain inside the folder `WEB-INF` from the `resteasy-examples` project. Let's create a file named `jboss-web. xml` with the following content:

```xml
<?xml version="1.0" encoding="UTF-8"?>
<jboss-web>
  <security-domain>other</security-domain>
</jboss-web>
```

Alright, let's configure the file web.xml in order to aggregate the security constraints. In the following block of code, you will see in bold what you should add:

```xml
<?xml version="1.0" encoding="UTF-8"?>
<web-app version="3.0" xmlns="http://java.sun.com/xml/ns/javaee"
   xmlns:xsi="http://www.w3.org/2001/XMLSchema-instance"
   xsi:schemaLocation="http://java.sun.com/xml/ns/javaee
   http://java.sun.com/xml/ns/javaee/web-app_3_0.xsd">
       <!-- Roles -->
   <security-role>
     <description>Any rol </description>
     <role-name>*</role-name>
   </security-role>

       <!-- Resource / Role Mapping -->
   <security-constraint>
     <display-name>Area secured</display-name>
     <web-resource-collection>
       <web-resource-name>protected_resources</web-resource-name>
       <url-pattern>/services/*</url-pattern>
       <http-method>GET</http-method>
       <http-method>POST</http-method>
     </web-resource-collection>
     <auth-constraint>
       <description>User with any role</description>
       <role-name>*</role-name>
     </auth-constraint>
   </security-constraint>

   <login-config>
     <auth-method>BASIC</auth-method>
   </login-config>
</web-app>
```

From a terminal, let's go to the home folder of the resteasy-examples project and execute mvn jboss-as:redeploy. Now, we will test our web service as we did in *Chapter 1, Setting Up the Environment,* using SOAP UI. We will perform a request using the POST method to the URL http://localhost:8080/resteasy-examples/services/person/ with the following XML:

```xml
<person><name>Rene</name><lastname>Enriquez</lastname></person>
```

We obtain the following response:

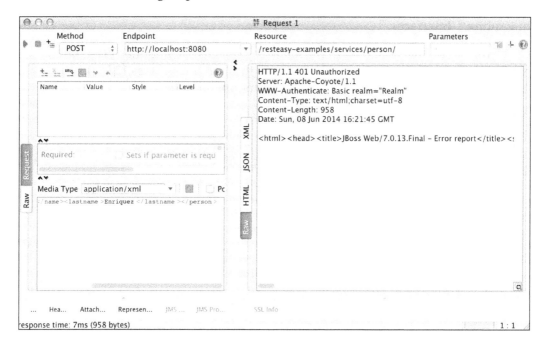

SOAP UI shows us the HTTP 401 error, which means that the request wasn't authorized. This is because we performed the request without delivering the credentials to the server. In order to do this, we have to click on the (**...**) button that is located in the left-bottom spot of SOAP UI and enter the user's credentials we just created, as shown in the following screenshot:

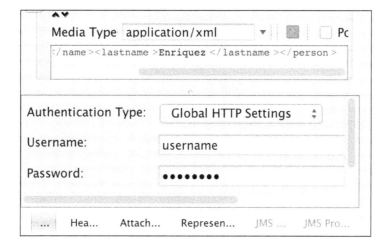

Now is the time to enable our traffic analyzer. Let's start Wireshark and set it to analyze the traffic inside the loopback address. From the **Main** menu, navigate to **Capture | Interfaces**.

Check the option **lo0**, as shown in the following screenshot, and then click on the **Start** button. This way, all traffic that goes through the address 127.0.0.1 or its equivalent localhost will be intercepted for our analysis.

Also, in the field `Filter`, we will type `http` just to intercept the HTTP request and response, as shown in the screenshot that follows later:

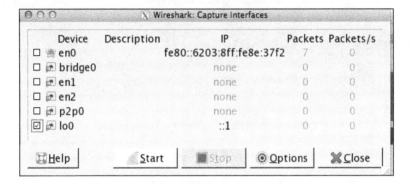

Have a look at the following screenshot:

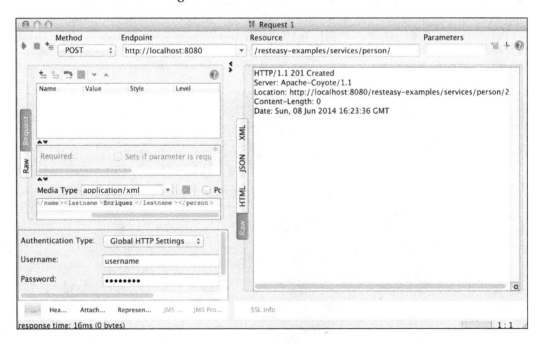

Once we have done this, we will perform the request operation from SOAP UI. Once again, SOAP UI shows us a HTTP 201 message; this time, the request is successfully processed. You can see the following columns of information in Wireshark:

- **No**: This column identifies the request or response in a unique way
- **Time**: This column identifies the time to execute the operation
- **Source**: This column identifies the address where requests/responses are originated
- **Destination**: This column identifies the target IP address to perform a HTTP request/response
- **Protocol**: This column identifies the protocol where requests/responses are performed
- **Length**: This column identifies the request/response length
- **Info**: This column identifies information related to the request/response

Now, it is time to watch the information traffic on Wireshark, as follows:

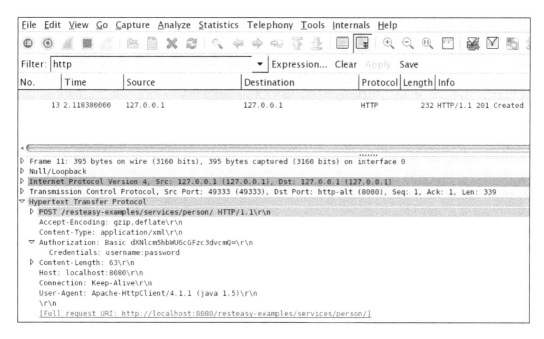

Notice how Wireshark shows us we are performing a POST (info) operation using the protocol HTTP with an XML string (protocol) to the target address 127.0.0.1 (destination). Also, you can read the username and password. Hence, this method is not very safe for security implementation because anyone can access this information and perform a phishing attack.

You can find the source code for this chapter at the following URL:

```
https://github.com/restful-java-web-services-security/source-code/
tree/master/chapter02/basic-authentication
```

Digest access authentication

This authentication method makes use of a hash function to encrypt the password entered by the user before sending it to the server. This, obviously, makes it much safer than the basic authentication method, in which the user's password travels in plain text that can be easily read by whoever intercepts it. To overcome such drawbacks, digest md5 authentication applies a function on the combination of the values of the username, realm of application security, and password. As a result, we obtain an encrypted string that can hardly be interpreted by an intruder.

To better understand this process, we will show you a simple explanation extracted from Wikipedia.

An example with explanation

The following example was originally given in RFC 2617 and is expanded here to show the full text expected for each request and response. Note that only the auth *(authentication) quality of protection code is covered — at the time of writing, only the Opera and Konqueror web browsers are known to support* auth-int *(authentication with integrity protection). Although the specification mentions HTTP Version 1.1, the scheme can be successfully added to the Version 1.0 server, as shown here.*

This typical transaction consists of the following steps:

The client asks for a page that requires authentication but does not provide a username and password. Typically, this is because the user simply entered the address or followed a link to the page.

The server responds with the 401 "Unauthorized" response code, providing the authentication realm and a randomly generated, single-use value called nonce.

At this point, the browser will present the authentication realm (typically, a description of the computer or system being accessed) to the user and prompt for a username and password. The user may decide to cancel at this point.

Once a username and password have been supplied, the client resends the same request but adds an authentication header that includes the response code.

In this example, the server accepts the authentication and the page is returned. If the username is invalid and/or the password is incorrect, the server might return the 401 response code and the client will prompt the user again.

A client may already have the required username and password without needing to prompt the user, for example, if they have previously been stored by a web browser.

If you want to know more about this mechanism, you can visit Wikipedia for the complete article following the link `http://en.wikipedia.org/wiki/Digest_access_authentication`.

You can also read the specification RFC 2617, which is available at `https://www.ietf.org/rfc/rfc2617.txt`.

Now, let's test this mechanism in our example.

In order to start, we must ensure that the environment variable JAVA_HOME is already set and added to the PATH variable. So, you can ascertain this by typing the following command in a terminal:

```
java -version
```

This will display the information shown in the following screenshot:

```
Last login: Wed Mar  5 22:19:50 on ttys000
MacBook-Pro-de-Rene:bin moe$ java -version
java version "1.7.0_45"
Java(TM) SE Runtime Environment (build 1.7.0_45-b18)
Java HotSpot(TM) 64-Bit Server VM (build 24.45-b08, mixed mode)
MacBook-Pro-de-Rene:bin moe$
```

This command shows us the Java version installed on our PC. In case you obtain an error instead of the previous output, you should create the environment variable JAVA_HOME, add it to the PATH variable, and repeat the verification.

Now, in order to perform what we explained before, we need to generate a password for our example user. We have to generate the password using the parameters we talked about earlier — username, realm, and password. Let's go to the directory of JBOSS_HOME/modules/org/picketbox/main/ from a terminal and type the following:

```
java -cp picketbox-4.0.7.Final.jar org.jboss.security.auth.callback.
RFC2617Digest username MyRealmName password
```

We will obtain the following result:

RFC2617 A1 hash: 8355c2bc1aab3025c8522bd53639c168

Through this process, we obtain the encrypted password and use it in our password storage file (the JBOSS_HOME/standalone/configuration/application-users. properties file). We must replace the password in the file, and it will be used for the user username. We have to replace it because the old password doesn't contain the realm name information of the application. As an alternative, you can create a new user using the file add-user.sh; you just have to deliver the realm information when you are requested.

In order to make our application work, we just need to make a little change in the web.xml file. We have to modify the auth-method tag, change the value FORM to DIGEST, and set the application realm name in the following way:

```
<login-config>


  <auth-method>DIGEST</auth-method>


  <realm-name>MyRealmName</realm-name>
</login-config>
```

Now, let's create a new security domain in JBoss so that we can manage the authentication mechanism `DIGEST`. On the `<security-domains>` section of the `JBOSS_HOME/standalone/configuration/standalone.xml` file, let's add the following entry:

```
<security-domain name="domainDigest" cache-type="default">
  <authentication>
    <login-module code="UsersRoles" flag="required">
      <module-option name="usersProperties" value="${jboss.server.
config.dir}/application-users.properties"/>
      <module-option name="rolesProperties" value="${jboss.server.
config.dir}/application-roles.properties"/>
      <module-option name="hashAlgorithm" value="MD5"/>
      <module-option name="hashEncoding" value="RFC2617"/>
      <module-option name="hashUserPassword" value="false"/>
      <module-option name="hashStorePassword" value="true"/>
      <module-option name="passwordIsA1Hash" value="true"/>
      <module-option name="storeDigestCallback"
        value="org.jboss.security.auth.callback.RFC2617Digest"/>
        </login-module>
  </authentication>
</security-domain>
```

Finally, in the application, change the security domain name in the file `jboss-web.xml`, as shown in the following code:

```
<?xml version="1.0" encoding="UTF-8"?>
<jboss-web>
  <security-domain>java:/jaas/domainDigest</security-domain>
</jboss-web>
```

We will change the authentication method from `BASIC` to `DIGEST` in the `web.xml` file. Also, we will enter the name of the security realm. All these changes must be applied in the tag `login-config` in the following way:

```
<login-config>
  <auth-method>DIGEST</auth-method>
  <realm-name>MyRealmName</realm-name>
</login-config>
```

Now, restart the application server and redeploy the application on JBoss. For this, execute the following command in the terminal command line:

```
mvn jboss-as:redeploy
```

Let's enable the catching of traffic through Wireshark and test the web service again using SOAP UI. First, we should change the field `Authentication Type` from Global HTTP Settings to **SPNEGO/Kerberos**. A very useful trick is to tell SOAP UI not to use the basic authentication method. Once we execute the request, Wireshark will tell us the message shown in the following screenshot:

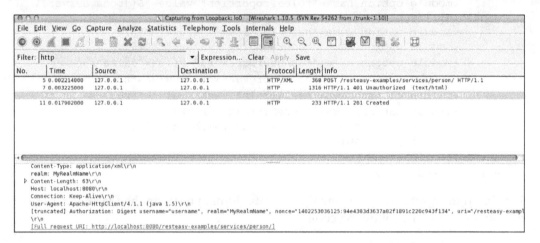

As shown in the screenshot, let's first confirm that all the steps described earlier are performed in this authentication method. Let's keep track using the **No** field in Wireshark:

In step 5, the request is performed.

In step 7, the server returns an error message code HTTP 401 with the generated `nonce` value. The `nonce` value helps to avoid replay attacks.

In step 9, the request is performed again. This time, the information required for authentication is included and all this information is encrypted in the same way we described earlier.

Finally, in step 11, we obtain the response that tells us the request has been successfully executed.

As you will notice, this is a more secure authentication method, mainly used if you don't want the overhead of full transport security through TLS/SSL encryption.

You can find the source code for this chapter at the following URL:

```
https://github.com/restful-java-web-services-security/source-code/
tree/master/chapter02/digest-authentication
```

Authentication through certificates

This is a mechanism in which a trust agreement is established between the server and the client through certificates. They must be signed by an agency established to ensure that the certificate presented for authentication is legitimate, which is known as CA.

Let's imagine an application that uses this mechanism of security. When the client attempts to access a protected resource, instead of providing a username or password, it presents the certificate to the server. This is the certificate that contains the user information for authentication; in other words, the credentials, besides a unique private-public key pair. The server determines if the user is legitimate through the CA. Then, it verifies whether the user has access to the resource. Also, you should know that this authentication mechanism must use HTTPS as the communication protocol as we don't have a secure channel and anyone could steal the client's identity.

Now, we will show how to do this in our example.

In our example, we turn ourselves into the CA; they are usually companies such as VERISIGN or others. However, as we want to save you money, we will do it this way. The first thing we need is a key for the CA (which is ourselves), and we will sign the certificates for the application server and users. As the purpose of this book is to explain how this method works and not how to generate certificates, we will not include all steps required to generate them, but we include them on GitHub at the following link:

```
https://github.com/restful-java-web-services-security/source-code/
tree/master/chapter02/client-cert-authentication
```

Alright, let's start. First, copy the `server.keystore` and `server.trutstore` files to the folder directory `JBOSS_HOME/standalone/configuration/`. You can download these files from GitHub using the following link:

```
https://github.com/restful-java-web-services-security/source-code/
tree/master/chapter02/client-cert-authentication/certificates
```

Now, as we mentioned before, this security mechanism requires our application server to use HTTPS as the communication protocol. So, we must enable HTTPS. Let's add a connector in the `standalone.xml` file; look for the following line:

```
<connector name="http"
```

Add the following block of code:

```
<connector name="https" protocol="HTTP/1.1" scheme="https" socket-
binding="https" secure="true">
  <ssl password="changeit"
certificate-key-file="${jboss.server.config.dir}/server.keystore"
verify-client="want"
ca-certificate-file="${jboss.server.config.dir}/server.truststore"/>

</connector>
```

Next, we add the security domain, as shown:

```
<security-domain name="RequireCertificateDomain">
                  <authentication>
    <login-module code="CertificateRoles" flag="required">
                          <module-option name="securityDomain" value
="RequireCertificateDomain"/>
                          <module-option name="verifier" value="org.
jboss.security.auth.certs.AnyCertVerifier"/>
                          <module-option name="usersProperties"
value="${jboss.server.config.dir}/my-users.properties"/>
                          <module-option name="rolesProperties"
value="${jboss.server.config.dir}/my-roles.properties"/>
                  </login-module>
  </authentication>
  <jsse keystore-password="changeit" keystore-
    url="file:${jboss.server.config.dir}/server.keystore"
                      truststore-password="changeit" truststore-
url="file:${jboss.server.config.dir}/server.truststore"/>
                  </security-domain>
```

As you can see, we need two files: `my-users.properties` and `my-roles.properties`; both are empty and located in the JBOSS_HOME/standalone/configuration path.

We will add the `<user-data-constraint>` tag in the `web.xml` file in the following way:

```
<security-constraint>
...<user-data-constraint>



  <transport-guarantee>CONFIDENTIAL</transport-guarantee>
  </user-data-constraint>
</security-constraint>
```

Then, change the authentication method to `CLIENT-CERT`, as shown:

```
<login-config>
  <auth-method>CLIENT-CERT</auth-method>
</login-config>
```

Finally, change the security domain in the `jboss-web.xml` file in the following way:

```
<?xml version="1.0" encoding="UTF-8"?>
<jboss-web>
  <security-domain>RequireCertificateDomain</security-domain>
</jboss-web>
```

Now, restart the application server and redeploy the application with Maven using the following command:

```
mvn jboss-as:redeploy
```

In order to test this authentication method, we will have to first perform some configurations in SOAP UI. First, let's go to the installation directory, find the file `vmoptions.txt`, and add the following line:

-Dsun.security.ssl.allowUnsafeRenegotiation=true

Now, we will change the SSL settings of SOAP UI. For this, you have to navigate to **File | Preferences** from the principal menu.

From the pop-up window, select the **SSL Settings** tab and enter the values shown in the following screenshot:

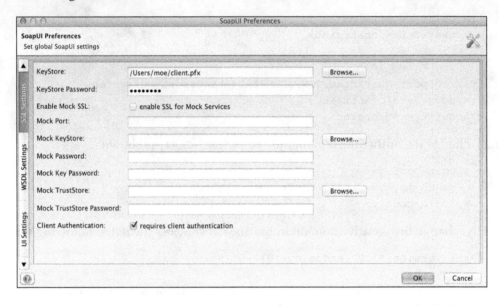

KeyStore is the place where you should have copied the .pfx file. Note that **KeyStore Password** is changeit and check the option **requires client authentication**.

Now, we will test the modifications we just did; so, let's enable the traffic analyzer and execute the request using SOAP UI again. Wireshark will show the information shown in the following screenshot:

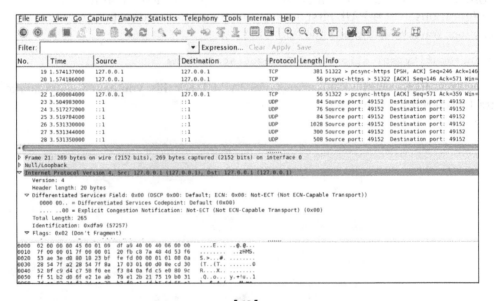

As you can see, all information is encrypted and it can't be interpreted. So, if the packages are transmitted and they are intercepted in the network, the information is not vulnerable to attacks.

You can find the source code of this section on GitHub at the following URL:

```
https://github.com/restful-java-web-services-security/source-code/
tree/master/chapter02/client-cert-authentication/resteasy-examples
```

API keys

With the advent of cloud computing, it is not difficult to think of applications that integrate with many others available in the cloud. Right now, it's easy to see how applications interact with Flickr, Facebook, Twitter, Tumblr, and so on.

To enable these integrations, a new authentication mechanism has been developed using API keys. This authentication method is used primarily when we need to authenticate from another application but we do not want to access the private user data hosted in another application. On the contrary, if you want to access this information, you must use OAuth. If you are interested in this, don't worry, we will study this wonderful technology later in this book.

We want to understand how the API keys work, so let's take the case of Flickr. The important thing here is to understand how the API keys work because the same concept can be applied to companies like Google, Facebook, and so on. For those unfamiliar with Flickr, it is an application in the cloud in which we can store our photos, images, screenshots, or similar files.

To start working with this authentication model, we first obtain an API key; in our example with Flickr, you can do this using the following link:

```
https://www.flickr.com/services/developer/api/
```

When we ask for our API key, we are asked to enter the name of the application that we will create and with which we use the API key. Once we enter the information requested and submit it, Flickr will deliver us a couple of values; they are a secret and a key. Both are displayed in the following screenshot:

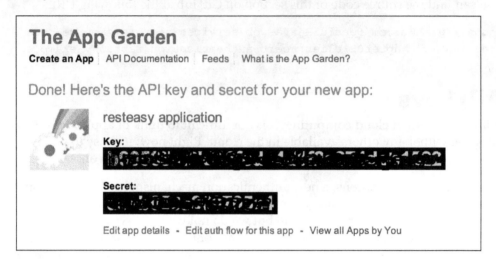

Each application we create is part of Flickr App Garden. App Garden is nothing but the set of all applications created by all Flickr members.

Keep in mind that when creating an API key, we consciously accept certain terms of use of the provider. These terms clearly detail what we can and can't do; for example, Flickr says:

a. You shall:

Comply with the Flickr Community Guidelines at www.flickr.com/ guidelines.gne, *the Flickr Terms of Use at* http://www.flickr.com/ terms.gne, *and the Yahoo! Terms of Service at* http://docs.yahoo.com/ info/terms/.

…

b. You shall not:

Use Flickr APIs for any application that replicates or attempts to replace the essential user experience of Flickr.com

…

Thus, by requiring that users accept the terms of use, API key providers prevent the abusive use of its APIs. So, if someone starts disrespecting agreements, the provider withdraws the API key. Flickr has a large set of methods that we can use in our applications; we will try one of them to show how they work:

The `flickr.photos.getRecent` method lists all recent photos that have been posted in Flickr, and we can invoke it as follows:

```
https://www.flickr.com/services/rest?method=flickr.photos.
getRecent&;&api+key=[your_api_key_from_flicker]
```

Let's use the key we just generated earlier, and let's perform the request using the browser as follows:

First notice how information travels through a secure channel (HTTPS). Then, when receiving the request, Flickr authenticates the user by reading the information from the API key with the secret key that belongs to the user. Once these validations are successful, the server delivers the response to the client. Thus, we obtain a response with all the photos that have been recently posted within Flickr. As you'll notice, this way, you can easily create applications using the provider's API. Also, the provider will allow you to authenticate, access public information, and be responsible to keep track of volume or the number of API calls you've made using the API key, in order to validate that the use complies with the agreements.

Summary

In this chapter, we went through all possible models of authentication. We will use all of them in the next chapter, and we will apply them to the web service functionality we just created.

Even if you had trouble with any of the examples, you can continue to the next chapter. As for your better understanding, we will go step-by-step and more in-depth into how we can leverage each available authentication model.

As you realize, it is important to choose the correct security management, otherwise information is exposed and can easily be intercepted and used by third parties.

Finally, in this chapter, we reviewed the differences between authentication and authorization. Both concepts are very important and definitely impossible to put aside in the context of security terms.

Now, we will ask you to join us to go ahead and secure our web service.

Security Management with RESTEasy

3

Welcome to the third chapter. We hope you are enjoying and learning with us. In this chapter, you will get more involved with security management. You will also work with some more advanced security concepts.

Security management in applications built with RESTful web services can be more granular than what we reviewed in the previous chapter. If we think around authentication and authorization topics, we described the former; authorization was set aside. This is because we want to treat it slowly and in a very detailed level in this chapter.

The topics covered in this chapter are:

- Implementing security restrictions related to authentication and authorization in to an application
- Implementing fine-grained security
- Using annotations to obtain more granularity over resource access control

Fine-grained and coarse-grained security

There are two levels of security we can manage: **fine-grained** and **coarse-grained**.

When we mention the term coarse-grained in the context of security, we refer to security systems that are generally handled at high levels within the application. The examples in *Chapter 2*, *The Importance of Securing Web Services*, in which a user with any role can make use of the services, is a perfect example of coarse-grained because the coarse-grained option is used when the security restrictions give access to users without worrying about roles or more specific features about the authenticated user. This means that in order for the system to allow access to functions, we just verify the user identity; in other words, it authenticates the user. However, it is not enough to have an authenticated user of the application in real life. It will also be necessary that the user is authorized to use certain features. We can achieve this using fine-grained controls. Validating the user's assigned permissions to access functions means using authorization controls.

To demonstrate these concepts in a practical way, we will make use of the application we created in the previous chapter. You can access the source code on GitHub at the following URL, under the basic authentication section:

```
https://github.com/restful-java-web-services-security/source-code/
tree/master/chapter02/basic-authentication
```

Let's start; suppose we want only users with the role `administrator` to be able to make use of the features in our application. The first thing to do is to change the `web.xml` file and add a constraint as follows. Note how the changes appear in bold:

```
<?xml version="1.0" encoding="UTF-8"?>
<web-app version="3.0" xmlns="http://java.sun.com/xml/ns/javaee"
  xmlns:xsi="http://www.w3.org/2001/XMLSchema-instance"
  xsi:schemaLocation="http://java.sun.com/xml/ns/javaee
  http://java.sun.com/xml/ns/javaee/web-app_3_0.xsd">

  <security-role>
    <description>Application roles</description>
    <role-name>administrator</role-name>
  </security-role>
  <security-constraint>
    <display-name>Area secured</display-name>
    <web-resource-collection>
      <web-resource-name>protected_resources</web-resource-name>
      <url-pattern>/services/*</url-pattern>
```

```
    </web-resource-collection>
    <auth-constraint>
      <description>User with administrator role</description>
  <role-name>administrator</role-name>
    </auth-constraint>
  </security-constraint>
  <login-config>
    <auth-method>BASIC</auth-method>
  </login-config>
</web-app>
```

Now, let's try to make the request using the user we just created (`username`). You will be surprised when you get a `403 Forbidden` error.

Note that if you try to make the request with invalid credentials, you will get the error `HTTP/1.1 401 Unauthorized`. The error is pretty clear; the access is unauthorized. This means that we have sent invalid credentials, and hence the user can't be authenticated. The error we just got is `HTTP/1.1 403 Forbidden`, which indicates that the user was successfully logged in but was not authorized to use the functionality that they require. This is demonstrated in the following screenshot:

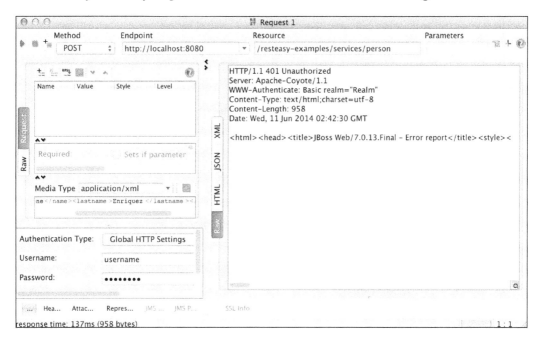

Now, let's create a new user with the role `administrator` using the `JBOSS_HOME/standalone/bin/adduser.sh` file. Enter the requested information as shown in the following screenshot:

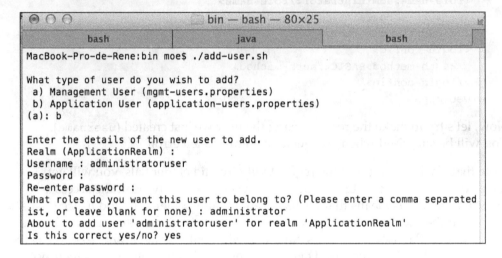

When we change the credentials in SoapUI, the result of the request is successful, as shown in the following screenshot:

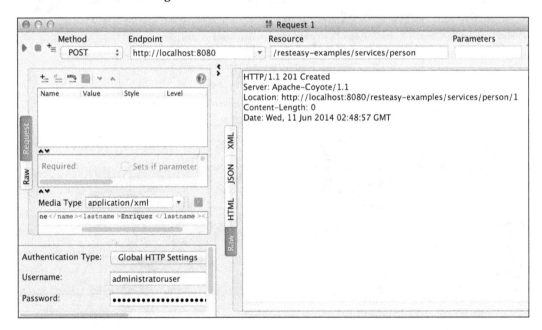

As you can see, we used an additional control in which we restricted only authenticated users with the `administrator` role assigned to them; they are capable of using the web service functions. It is very common to use these kinds of controls when managing security on real-world applications. As we have implemented a more detailed level of control, the platform offers us the opportunity to implement more granular controls, such as the ones we will see right now.

Securing HTTP methods

One of the benefits of JAAS is that we have control even at the level of HTTP methods. Thus, we can implement security controls to allow only users with a certain role to use certain methods with regards to our convenience; for example, one role to save information, another to delete it, others to read it, and so on.

To implement these kinds of controls, it is necessary that we understand the HTTP methods' functionality in the application. In our example, we already know that in order to save information, the application always uses the HTTP POST method. Also, when we want to read information, the application uses the HTTP GET method. Therefore, we will modify our example so that only users with the `administrator` role are able to use the `savePerson` (HTTP POST) method. Meanwhile, only those with the `reader` role will be able to read information using the `findById` (HTTP GET) method.

With this as our objective, we will modify our `web.xml` file as follows:

```
<?xml version="1.0" encoding="UTF-8"?>
<web-app version="3.0" xmlns="http://java.sun.com/xml/ns/javaee"
  xmlns:xsi="http://www.w3.org/2001/XMLSchema-instance"
xsi:schemaLocation="http://java.sun.com/xml/ns/javaee
  http://java.sun.com/xml/ns/javaee/web-app_3_0.xsd">
  <!-- Roles -->
  <security-role>
    <description>Role for save information</description>
    <role-name>administrator</role-name>
  </security-role>
  <security-role>
    <description>Role for read information</description>
    <role-name>reader</role-name>
  </security-role>

  <!-- Resource / Role Mapping -->
  <security-constraint>
    <display-name>Administrator area</display-name>
    <web-resource-collection>
<web-resource-name>protected_resources</web-resource-name>
      <url-pattern>/services/*</url-pattern>
      <http-method>POST</http-method>
```

```
      </web-resource-collection>
      <auth-constraint>
      <description>User with administrator role</description>
        <role-name>administrator</role-name>
      </auth-constraint>
    </security-constraint>
    <security-constraint>
      <display-name>Reader area</display-name>
      <web-resource-collection>
    <web-resource-name>protected_resources</web-resource-name>
        <url-pattern>/services/*</url-pattern>
        <http-method>GET</http-method>
      </web-resource-collection>
      <auth-constraint>
        <description>User with reader role</description>
        <role-name>reader</role-name>
      </auth-constraint>
    </security-constraint>

    <login-config>
      <auth-method>BASIC</auth-method>
    </login-config>
  </web-app>
```

Before we continue, we must create a new user (`readeruser`) with the role `reader` using the `JBOSS_HOME/standalone/bin/adduser.sh` script.

Now, let's test the roles and their permissions using SoapUI.

HTTP method – POST

We are going to test the `POST` method using a role that doesn't have the required permissions. You will see the permission error message.

Role: Reader

This method is not allowed when using this role. This is demonstrated in the following screenshot:

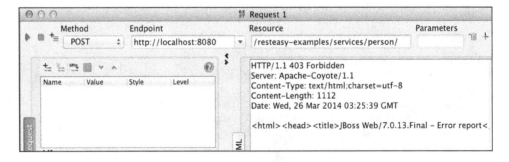

Role: Administrator

With this role, you can execute the method successfully. This is demonstrated in the following screenshot:

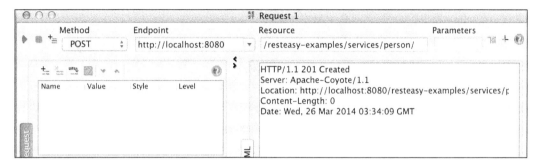

HTTP method – GET

Now, we are going to use a user with the required permissions to use the GET method. The execution should be successful with this role.

Role: Reader

Now, the execution is successful with this role. This is demonstrated in the following screenshot:

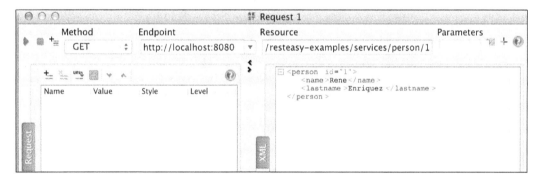

Role: Administrator

The admin role does not have access to this method. This is demonstrated in the following screenshot:

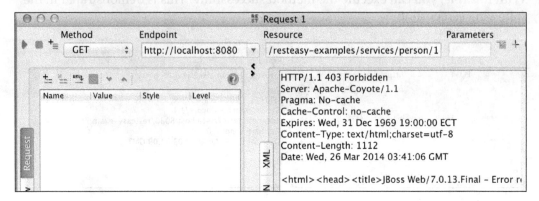

The same consideration of roles can be used for URL patterns. In our example, we apply the restriction on the `/services/*` pattern. However, you can apply it at a deeper level, for example `/services/person/*`. We mean that if we had another service that is exposed under the URL `/services/other-service/`, we can set it so that a role has access to services under the path `/services/person/*` and different levels of access under the path `/services/other-service/*`. This example is quite simple and is proposed as a basic example to the reader.

After applying all the changes, we set security over all methods listed in the `web.xml` file. However, we must ask ourselves a question; what happens with the methods that haven't been included?

The OWASP (Open Web Application Security Project), a nonprofit organization dedicated to finding and fixing security holes in software, has written a paper on this, and it is called the following:

> *Bypassing Web Authentication and Authorization with HTTP Verb Tampering: How to inadvertently allow attackers full access to your web application.*

If you want to check out the complete document, you can do so by accessing the following link:

`http://dl.packetstormsecurity.net/papers/web/Bypassing_VBAAC_with_HTTP_Verb_Tampering.pdf`

What the OWASP describes in the aforementioned document is simple. It shows that JEE exposes potential security gaps in the `web.xml` configuration file if we don't take certain precautions as all methods that are not listed in the file can be used without any restrictions. This means that a user that hasn't been authenticated in the application can invoke any other HTTP method.

The OWASP states the following in the earlier article:

> *Unfortunately, almost all the implementations of this mechanism work in an*
> *unexpected and insecure war. Rather than denying methods not specified in the*
> *rule, they allow any method not listed. Ironically, by listing specific methods in*
> *their rule, developers are actually allowing more access than they intended.*

In order to understand this in a better way, let's focus on an analogy.

Suppose you have a web application to write books that handles two roles—one for authors who are able to write the pages of the books and another for reviewers who can only read the books and add notes with comments. Now, suppose a user ends up getting the URL of your application by mistake. This user does not have any credentials to deliver, and the obvious thing is that the user should not even be able to access the application. However, the problem that is demonstrated by the OWASP is that instead of doing what seems obvious, it actually enables application access to unauthenticated users with enough permission to perform any operation on the books, such as removing them.

Let's take an example in order to see this inconvenience, and after that, we will implement OWASP's suggestions to solve it.

Let's create a new method within the class `PersonService`; we'll use one of the methods that has not been listed in the `web.xml` file this time. One of the most used methods is `HTTP DELETE`; its functionality is to remove one of the entries stored in memory using its ID. This will pass the ID of the record as a parameter in the URL, so the URL of the request will look like the following:

```
http://localhost:8080/resteasy-examples/services/person/[ID]
```

The method implementation should look like the following:

```
@DELETE
@Path("{id}")
public Response delete(@PathParam("id") int id) {
  Person person = dataInMemory.get(id);
if (person == null) {
  // There is no person with this ID
throw new WebApplicationException(Response.Status.NOT_FOUND);
  }
  dataInMemory.remove(id);
  return Response.status(Status.GONE).build();
}
```

In order to test the method, we must first create a couple of registers through SoapUI, also using the `HTTP POST` method and a string such as the following:

```
<person><name>Rene</name><lastname>Enriquez</lastname></person>
```

Now, select the `DELETE` method in SoapUI, remove the information on the credentials we use for authentication, and perform a request using one of the item IDs, as shown in the following screenshot:

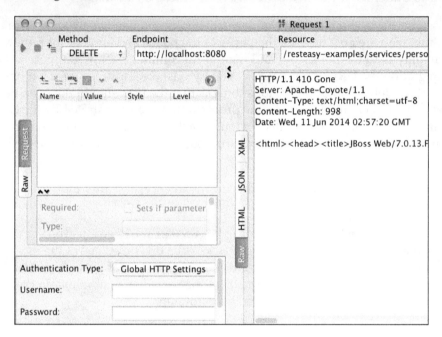

As you can see, the item was removed and the server returns the message `HTTP/1.1 410 Gone`. This indicates that the resource is no longer available. As you have noted, when we don't specify that this method should be protected by default, it is marked as available. In our case, any user without the need to authenticate can remove our application resources.

To overcome this drawback, the OWASP recommends adding another security constraint in the `web.xml` file. This new security constraint should not have any HTTP method listed within itself, which means denying access to all HTTP methods, as shown in the following code:

```
<security-constraint>
  <display-name>For any user</display-name>
  <web-resource-collection>
  <web-resource-name>protected_resources</web-resource-name>
    <url-pattern>/services/*</url-pattern>
```

```
      </web-resource-collection>
      <auth-constraint>
        <description>User with any role</description>
        <role-name>*</role-name>
      </auth-constraint>
    </security-constraint>
```

Also, we will have to add a new role in order to determine an authenticated user in the application, as shown in the following code:

```
    <security-role>
        <description>Any role</description>
        <role-name>*</role-name>
    </security-role>
```

Now, we run the request from SoapUI, and we can see the error message `HTTP/1.1 401 Unauthorized`. This indicates that you cannot execute the request because the user has not been authenticated, which in turn means that unauthenticated users cannot use the `DELETE` or any other method.

Fine-grained security implementation through annotations

The `web.xml` file, the file that allows all security settings, is not the only way in which you can achieve fine-grained security implementation; the platform also offers the possibility of using annotations for security checks. To do this, there are three options that can be chosen depending on your needs, listed as follows:

- `@RolesAllowed`
- `@DenyAll`
- `@PermitAll`

The @RolesAllowed annotation

The `@RolesAllowed` annotation can be applied at the method or class level. With this annotation, you can define a set of roles that are allowed to use the annotated resource. As a parameter annotation, let's write all allowed roles. For this example, we will modify our `web.xml` file as follows:

```
    <?xml version="1.0" encoding="UTF-8"?>
    <web-app version="3.0" xmlns="http://java.sun.com/xml/ns/javaee"
      xmlns:xsi="http://www.w3.org/2001/XMLSchema-instance"
    xsi:schemaLocation="http://java.sun.com/xml/ns/javaee
      http://java.sun.com/xml/ns/javaee/web-app_3_0.xsd">
```

```
<!-- Roles -->
<context-param>
  <param-name>resteasy.role.based.security</param-name>
  <param-value>true</param-value>
</context-param>
<security-role>
  <description>Any role</description>
  <role-name>*</role-name>
</security-role>
<!-- Resource / Role Mapping -->
<security-constraint>
<display-name>Area for authenticated users</display-name>
  <web-resource-collection>
<web-resource-name>protected_resources</web-resource-name>
    <url-pattern>/services/*</url-pattern>
  </web-resource-collection>
  <auth-constraint>
    <description>User with any role</description>
    <role-name>*</role-name>
  </auth-constraint>
</security-constraint>
<login-config>
  <auth-method>BASIC</auth-method>
</login-config>
</web-app>
```

In the class `PersonService`, let's use the annotation on every method with the roles we want to be able to execute the method, as follows:

```
@RolesAllowed({ "reader", "administrator" })
@POST
@Consumes("application/xml")
public Response savePerson(Person person) {...

@RolesAllowed({ "administrator" })
@GET
@Path("{id}")
@Produces("application/xml")
public Person findById(@PathParam("id") int id) {...
```

It is now time to test it through SoapUI.

The savePerson method

Now, we will test the `savePerson` method of the `PersonService` class with the admin role, as shown in the following screenshot:

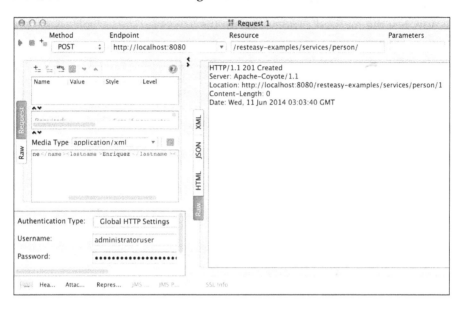

The execution was successful, as you can see in the preceding screenshot. The reason is because we included both roles in the `@RolesAllowed` annotation. Also, we will test the execution using the `reader` role for it to be successful, as shown in the following screenshot:

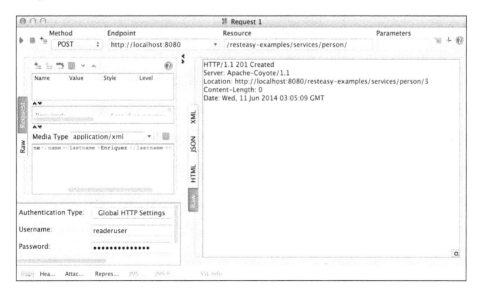

As you can see, we grant permissions to specific roles when we use the annotation @ RolesAllowed. For this method, we used administrator and reader.

The findById method

We will now test the method findById with the administrator role, as shown in the following screenshot:

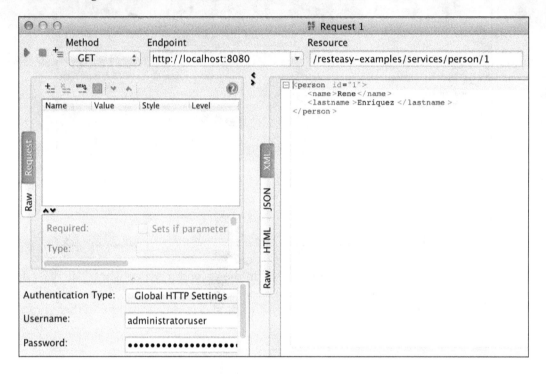

The screenshot shows that the execution was successful because the @RolesAllowed annotation includes admin. As we didn't include the reader role, the next execution should not be authorized. Let's test it right now, as shown in the following screenshot:

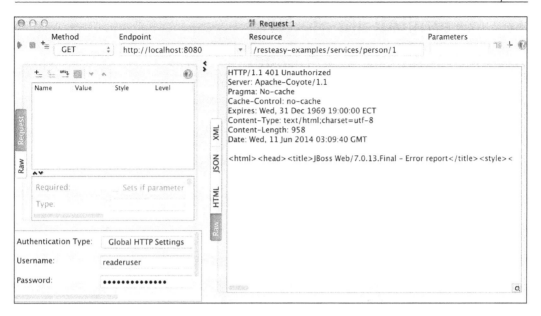

Once again, we used the annotation `@RolesAllowed` to grant permissions at a method level, but this time we specified just one role, `administrator`.

All the source code for this chapter can be found at the following URL:

`https://github.com/restful-java-web-services-security/source-code/tree/master/chapter03`

The @DenyAll annotation

The `@DenyAll` annotation allows us to define operations that cannot be invoked regardless of whether the user is authenticated or the roles are related to the user. The specification defines this annotation as follows:

Specifies that no security roles are allowed to invoke the specified method(s) - i.e. that the methods are to be excluded from execution in the J2EE container.

The @PermitAll annotation

When we use the @PermitAll annotation, we tell the container that the annotated resource (a method or all methods of the class) can be invoked by any user who has logged in to the application. This means that it is only necessary that the user be authenticated; it's not required to have any specific role assigned.

From these three annotations, the most used is undoubtedly the first one (@RolesAllowed); the others aren't often used since @PermitAll can be easily replaced in the web.xml file, and @DenyAll can be used only in few scenarios.

Programmatical implementation of fine-grained security

RESTEasy, besides providing options for security management that we have seen, programmatically provides an additional mechanism for access control.

Within the operations of web services, you can add an additional parameter to the method. This allows access to the security context, without altering the way clients invoke the method or the action that the method executes. The parameter must be included in the following way:

```
@GET...
@Consumes("text/xml")
public returnType methodName(@Context SecurityContext secContext, …)
{...
```

Suppose that in our example, in the method savePerson, we want access to this functionality. The only change we need to make is shown in the following code snippets.

Earlier, the method used just one parameter, as shown in the following code:

```
@POST
@Consumes("application/xml")
public Response savePerson(Person person) {
    int id = dataInMemory.size() + 1;
    person.setId(id);
    dataInMemory.put(id, person);
    return Response.created(URI.create("/person/" + id)).build();
}
```

Now, the method has another parameter, as shown in the following code:

```
@POST
@Consumes("application/xml")
public Response savePerson(@Context SecurityContext secContext,
  Person person) {
  int id = dataInMemory.size() + 1;
  person.setId(id);
  dataInMemory.put(id, person);
  return Response.created(URI.create("/person/" + id)).build();
}
```

The interface `javax.ws.rs.core.SecurityContext` offers the following three interesting features:

- `isUserInRole()`

- `getUserPrincipal()`

- `isSecure()`

The functionality of the method `isUserInRole ()` is similar to the annotation `@RolesAllowed`; its goal is to perform a check in order to determine if a logged user belongs to a specified role, as follows:

```
@POST
@Consumes("application/xml")
public Response savePerson(@Context SecurityContext secContext,
  Person person) {
  boolean isInDesiredRole =   secContext.isUserInRole
    ("NameOfDesiredRole");
  int id = dataInMemory.size() + 1;
  person.setId(id);
  dataInMemory.put(id, person);
  return Response.created(URI.create("/person/" + id)).build();
}
```

The `getUserPrincipal()` method obtains the primary user in the application, in other words, the logged user. You can obtain information such as the username that represents it through this user; this is always useful in scenarios in which you want to generate audit trails.

Finally, the method `isSecure()` determines whether the invocation is being made through a secure means of communication, such as whether you are using HTTPS.

As you know, HTTP and HTTPS are protocols to exchange information; the former is usually used when you share information that is not sensitive, and the latter is often used when the information is sensitive and we need a secure channel.

Let's imagine the web portal of ABC Bank, particularly the home page where it shows information about services and stuff related to the bank's business that can be managed with HTTP. We can't manage the web pages that work with information about accounts or money transfers with the HTTP protocol; this is because the information is not protected. Through the HTTPS protocol, we can encrypt the information; when the information is intercepted by a traffic analyzer such as Wireshark, it can't be interpreted.

This functionality can be tested by applying the changes to the project to enable HTTPS, as we show you in *Chapter 2*, *The Importance of Securing Web Services*.

When you invoke this method using HTTP, the result will be false, but it will be true when you invoke the same method using HTTPS.

These three methods we just analyzed are very useful when we want to implement fine-grained security checks. For example, when we want to implement an audit, we can determine if one action was executed using a transmission secure protocol such as HTTPS; also, we can discover information about the user that is executing the action.

Summary

The needs that we have when implementing application security can be quite varied. In this chapter, we saw how JAX-RS offers mechanisms to handle security, starting from a fairly basic model (coarse-grained) to a more elaborate one (fine-grained) in which you can perform more exhaustive controls, including programmatic controls and controls through configuration files.

Of course, it is always recommended to keep these checks in configuration files such as `web.xml`. Since you have the controls centralized in one place, it facilitates maintenance. This does not occur when security is handled at the level of source code, because when there are many classes that are part of the project, the tasks get complicated when some form of modification to the current functionality is required.

Now, you should prepare for the next chapter, in which we will talk about OAuth. It's a very exciting topic because this protocol is widely accepted and used across Internet applications. The rockstar companies of the World Wide Web, such as Google, Twitter, and Facebook, among others, use it with great success.

4
RESTEasy Skeleton Key

Welcome to the fourth chapter! We hope you are enjoying the book, and even more important, learning and understanding what we are transmitting and teaching you. It is time to move forward and immerse yourself in a new chapter.

Once you read this chapter, you will have the knowledge to design, implement, and aggregate additional security levels to your RESTEasy applications, all of this using OAuth and RESTEasy Skeleton Key and some other specific requirements of these technologies, such as setting up an OAuth server. You will learn through practical and descriptive examples of applications, just as we did in previous chapters; we won't get stuck in theory only, and we'll implement applications and explain specific methods and classes to implement OAuth.

In this chapter, you will learn about the following topics:

- OAuth and RESTEasy
- SSO configuration for security management
- Access tokens
- Custom filters
- Web services clients for test

As you have probably experienced, if you have an account on one or several social networks, a lot of these social networks allow you to share information between them or post something in all of them. This is a sign that applications need to share information and also use resources that are in other applications. In this example, it can be your account or your contact list. This involves sensitive information, so it needs to be protected. Also, limited permissions over resources means that a third-party application can only read your contacts list. This opens the door to a very important, attractive, and useful feature among applications, which is the capacity to use resources on behalf of the user. Of course, you may ask how the latter authorizes the use? Well, this chapter will show you. So, let's go!

OAuth protocol

This is an open protocol that allows you to grant safe authorization to your private resources from one site (service provider) to another (consumer) without sharing your identity.

A practical example is when you grant authorization to a website or an application to use the contact list in your phone or social network.

OAuth and RESTEasy Skeleton Key

In this section, we will review some concepts related to OAuth as an authentication framework, RESTEasy Skeleton Key, and how they work together. You will check out some features of these technologies and get your hands dirty with some code as a practical example.

What is RESTEasy Skeleton Key?

RESTEasy Skeleton Key provides a unified way for browser and JAX-RS clients to be secured. This allows executing and forwarding requests in a network of applications and services in a secure and scalable way, without interacting with a central authentication server every time a request appears.

OAuth 2.0 authentication framework

This enables third-party applications or services access to an HTTP resource on behalf of the resource owner. It also prevents the third-party application or service from getting in contact with the owner's credentials. This is possible through issuing access tokens via browsers and using a direct grant.

With the two concepts explained in a nutshell, it is time to describe how they are related. RESTEasy Skeleton Key is an OAuth 2.0 implementation that uses the JBoss AS 7 security infrastructure in order to secure web applications and RESTful services.

This means that you can transform a web application into an OAuth 2.0 access token provider, and you can also transform the JBoss AS 7 security domain into a central authentication and authorization server, where applications and services can interact with each other.

The following diagram describes this process in a better way:

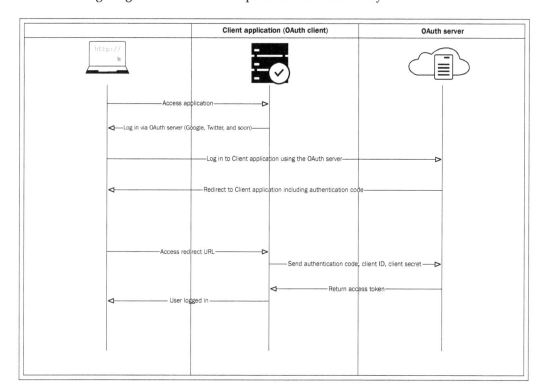

Main features

We want to help you understand these technologies and clarify what they are used for; this is why we will name some of their main features. With OAuth 2.0 and RESTEasy Skeleton Key, you can perform the following functions:

- Transform a servlet-form-auth-based web application into an OAuth 2.0 provider.

- Provide distributed **Single Sign-On (SSO)** throughout a central authentication server in order to log in once and access any browser-based application configured in the domain in a secure way.

- Use just one link and log out from all the distributed applications that were configured with SSO.

- Make a web application interact with a remote RESTful service using access tokens.

- Sign access tokens with OAuth 2.0 and use the tokens later to access any service configured in the domain. The token has Identity and Role Mapping, and there is no need to overload the central authentication server with every request that appears because tokens are digitally signed.

You can find more information about these topics at `http://docs.jboss.org/ resteasy/docs/3.0-beta-2/userguide/html/oauth2.html`.

We will discuss the most important parts, but it might be useful for you.

OAuth2 implementation

We have just reviewed some of the main concepts that we will deal with in this chapter, but this is not enough. We must implement a descriptive example so that we can completely understand these topics.

Updating RESTEasy modules in JBoss

In order not to mess with your JBoss configuration or anything else, we will use another brand new instance of JBoss. We have to update some modules that are related to RESTEasy. We can do this very easily. Let's visit the link `http://resteasy.jboss.org/`; at your right, you will find a panel with the title **Useful Links**, which has a download link. Click on it to visit another page that has a bunch of download links. In this example, we use the 3.0.7.Final Version. Download this version in order to go forward.

Once you have downloaded and unzipped it, you will find another `.zip` file named `resteasy-jboss-modules-3.0.7.Final`; this file contains some JARs that will update your JBoss modules. So, unzip it, copy all folders into `JBOSS_HOME/modules/`, and replace all coincidences. There is one last step: we have to update the JAR files' version and modify the module XML in JBoss in order to set `org.apache.httpcomponents` to use `httpclient-4.2.1.jar`, `httpcore-4.2.1.jar` and `httpmime-4.2.1.jar` because the current latest Version is 4.3.4, which works fine too. So, copy these JARs and update the version in the `module.xml` file in `JBOSS_HOME/modules/org/apache` folder. Now, we have updated our modules for RESTEasy.

Setting up the configuration in JBoss

For the next step in getting our JBoss ready for our example, we must go to `https://github.com/restful-java-web-services-security/source-code/tree/master/chapter04` and download the `chapter04` examples zip file. Unzip and you will find a folder named `configuration`. This folder contains the files necessary for setting up our JBoss configuration. So, copy the files and replace the configuration folder in your JBoss located at `JBOSS_HOME/standalone/configuration`.

Implementing an OAuth client

In order to develop this example, we investigate a very useful example and apply it to a new project. This example is composed of several projects; each project will produce a WAR file. The purpose of this example is to demonstrate how OAuth works and explain the way you can implement this technology at a technical level. So, we will simulate several things in order to create the environment where we can apply this implementation. The complete code can be downloaded from the following link:

`https://github.com/restful-java-web-services-security/source-code/tree/master/chapter04/oauth2-as7-example`

The oauth-client project

First we are going to create the `oauth-client` webapp project. You can use the Maven command we have used before in previous chapters or you can use Eclipse IDE in order to perform this.

After that, let's add some dependencies in order to implement our client. These dependencies are for all the projects. Go to the `pom.xml` file and make sure to add the following dependencies inside the `<dependencies>` tag:

```
<dependency>
        <groupId>org.jboss.spec.javax.servlet</groupId>
        <artifactId>jboss-servlet-api_3.0_spec</artifactId>
        <version>1.0.1.Final</version>
        <scope>provided</scope>
    </dependency>
    <dependency>
        <groupId>org.jboss.resteasy</groupId>
        <artifactId>resteasy-client</artifactId>
        <version>3.0.6.Final</version>
        <scope>provided</scope>
    </dependency>
    <dependency>
        <groupId>org.jboss.resteasy</groupId>
```

```
        <artifactId>skeleton-key-core</artifactId>
        <version>3.0.6.Final</version>
        <scope>provided</scope>
    </dependency>
```

Let's start by creating the package com.packtpub.resteasy.example.oauth. Then, create the class public class Loader implements ServletContextListener, which implements ServletContextListener, because we will load a key store and initialize a context.

Let's add a field into our class private ServletOAuthClient oauthClient, which will represent our OAuth client object.

Then, let's create the method shown in the following piece of code:

```
private static KeyStore loadKeyStore(String filename, String password)
throws Exception
{
KeyStore keyStore =
  KeyStore.getInstance(KeyStore.getDefaultType());
File keyStoreFile = new File(filename);
FileInputStream keyStoreStream = new
  FileInputStream(keyStoreFile);
    keyStore.load(keyStoreStream, password.toCharArray());
    keyStoreStream.close();
    return keyStore;
}
```

This method receives two parameters, the filename and the password, and creates the object KeyStore. It also creates a FileInputStream object from the filename received so that it can use it to load the KeyStore object, and it uses the password received in the form of a char array.

After this, as our class implements the ServletContextListener interface, we have to override some methods. The first method to override is contextInitialized. Let's do it as follows:

```
@Override
 public void contextInitialized(ServletContextEvent sce) {
   String truststoreKSPath = "${jboss.server.config.dir}/client-
truststore.ts";
   String truststoreKSPassword = "changeit";
   truststoreKSPath = EnvUtil.replace(truststoreKSPath);
   try {
    KeyStore truststoreKS = loadKeyStore(truststoreKSPath,
      truststoreKSPassword);
```

```
    oauthClient = new ServletOAuthClient();
    oauthClient.setTruststore(truststoreKS);
    oauthClient.setClientId("third-party");
    oauthClient.setPassword("changeit");
    oauthClient.setAuthUrl("https://localhost:8443/oauth-server/login.
jsp");
    oauthClient.setCodeUrl("https://localhost:8443/oauth-server/
      j_oauth_resolve_access_code");
    oauthClient.start();
    sce.getServletContext().setAttribute(ServletOAuthClient.class.
getName(), oauthClient);
  } catch (Exception e) {
  throw new RuntimeException(e);
  }


}
```

Through this method, we will accomplish several things. As you can see, we set two internal variables; one is set with the path to our `client-truststore.ts` file and the other is set to the password. Make sure to paste the file in the path we specified in the variable (`JBOSS_HOME/standalone/configuration`).

After this, we load the `KeyStore` object using the path and password we specified in the variables, obtaining another `KeyStore` object through this.

Now, it's time to instantiate and set the properties of our OAuth client object. In the previous code, we set the following properties: `trustStore`, `clientId`, `password`, `authUrl`, and `codeUrl`.

Finally, we create the client to obtain an access token from the code. In order to accomplish this, we use the `start()` method. Also, we set the attribute servlet OAuth client with the OAuth client object we just created.

In order to finish our OAuth client, we need to override a second method named `public void contextDestroyed(ServletContextEvent sce)`, as shown in the following code:

```
@Override
  public void contextDestroyed(ServletContextEvent sce) {
    oauthClient.stop();
  }
```

This method will be executed when the servlet context is about to shut down, our application is redeploying, and so on. The method closes the client instance and all its associated resources.

We implemented our OAuth client for our example. We need another resource. This time, we will create a class that works as a database client for our compact discs store. So, let's name it `CompactDiscsDatabaseClient`, and we will get the two following methods:

- `public static void redirect(HttpServletRequest request, HttpServletResponse response)`
- `public static List<String> getCompactDiscs(HttpServletRequest request)`

So, let's begin implementing the first method. This method is explained as follows:

```
public static void redirect(HttpServletRequest request,
  HttpServletResponse response) {
ServletOAuthClient oAuthClient = (ServletOAuthClient) request.
getServletContext().getAttribute(ServletOAuthClient.class.
  getName());
    try {
oAuthClient.redirectRelative("discList.jsp", request, response);
    } catch (IOException e) {
      throw new RuntimeException(e);
    }
  }
```

In the preceding method, we obtain the `ServletOAuthClient` object from the `ServletContext` obtained from the request; the servlet OAuth client is in the servlet context as an attribute named `ServletOAuthClient`. Remember that in the first class we created, we set this attribute in the servlet context.

Finally, we start the process of getting an access token by redirecting the browser to the authentication server through `redirectRelative (String relativePath, HttpServletRequest request, HttpServletResponse response)`.

Now, let's move on with the next method that loads the discs. The following code represents the method:

```
public static List<String> getCompactDiscs(HttpServletRequest request)
{

ServletOAuthClient oAuthClient = (ServletOAuthClient) request.
getServletContext().getAttribute(
        ServletOAuthClient.class.getName());

ResteasyClient rsClient = new
```

```
ResteasyClientBuilder().trustStore(oAuthClient.getTruststore())
  .hostnameVerification(ResteasyClientBuilder.
HostnameVerificationPolicy.ANY).build();

String urlDiscs = "https://localhost:8443/store/discs";
  try {
String bearerToken = "Bearer" + oAuthClient.getBearerToken(request);

Response response = rsClient.target(urlDiscs).request().
header(HttpHeaders.AUTHORIZATION, bearerToken)
        .get();
    return response.readEntity(new GenericType<List<String>>() {
        });
    } finally {
      rsClient.close();
    }
}
```

Let's check what we have up here. In the preceding getCompactDiscs () method, we create a ServletOAuthClient object that is in charge of starting the process of obtaining an access token by redirecting the browser to the authentication server. Once again, we obtain the attribute from the ServletContext object from the request. Then, we create a ResteasyClient object using a new instance of ResteasyClientBuilder(); this class is an abstraction to create clients and allows SSL configuration.

We then set the client-side trust store with the trustStore() method. This invocation will return a KeyStore object and set the client-side trust store. After this, we invoke the hostnameVerification() method, which sets an SSL policy used to verify hostnames. Finally, using the build() method, we build a new client instance with the entire configuration previously specified in this client builder. This will return an instance of ResteasyClient.

Let's move on to create an internal variable which will hold the URL of the resource that we will set as our target resource. Also, we will create another internal variable to hold the bearer token as a string. This string will comprise the word Bearer followed by the bearer token from the servlet OAuth client and request.

Now, in order to create the response, we will use the servlet OAuth client we just created. Let's use the variable urlDiscs as a parameter and create a new web resource target through the target() method. After this, using the request() method, we set up a request to the targeted web resource we just set.

Finally, we add a header by invoking the `header()` method, which will receive two parameters: the first parameter represents the header's name and the second parameter is the header's value. After this, we invoke the `HTTP GET` method for the current request.

Just to clarify, the `HttpHeaders.AUTHORIZATION` constant represents the header field in the specific case when a user wants to authenticate themselves with a server. It does so by adding an authorization request-header field along with the request. On the other hand, the authorization field value is composed of credentials that contain the authentication information of the user for the realm of the resource being requested.

Once the response object is created, we use the `readEntity()` method to read the message entity input stream as an instance of the specified Java type. With this, we fill the list with our compact discs example list so that we can present it in the web page. This means that we accessed the resource.

If you want to explore more about what we just used in the block of code we described, here are some links as references. You can check them out, expand your knowledge, and get more details on `RestEasyClient` and `RestEasyClientBuilder`:

- `http://www.w3.org/Protocols/rfc2616/rfc2616-sec14.html`
- `http://docs.jboss.org/resteasy/docs/3.0.2.Final/javadocs/org/jboss/resteasy/client/jaxrs/ResteasyClient.html`
- `http://docs.jboss.org/resteasy/docs/3.0.1.Final/javadocs/org/jboss/resteasy/client/jaxrs/ResteasyClientBuilder.html#truststore`

The discstore project

The next project we are going to create is the `discstore` project; the steps to create the project are the same as the previous one, and you can use the Maven command or Eclipse IDE.

In this project, we will create a class that will create the list of compact discs. This class is pretty simple, and it uses some annotations that have already been discussed in previous chapters. The name of this class will be `CompactDiscService`, and it will have only one method with several annotations. Let's start with the code, and we will add a short description about it after the code block:

```
@Path("discs")
public class CompactDiscService {
  @GET
  @Produces("application/json")
  public List<String> getCompactDiscs() {
```

```
    ArrayList<String> compactDiscList = new ArrayList<String>();
    compactDiscList.add("The Ramones");
    compactDiscList.add("The Clash");
    compactDiscList.add("Nirvana");
    return compactDiscList;
  }
}
```

As you can see, the method `getCompactDiscs()` is in charge of creating a list of strings, which each item will represent as a compact disc as this is an example in which we will add three items.

The `@Produces` annotations are used to specify the MIME media types, and if applied at the method level, the annotations override any `@Produces` annotation applied at the class level. The `@GET` annotation, as you already know, will represent the HTTP method `GET`. Meanwhile, the `@Path` annotation will help us to set the class as a resource, and its name will be `discs`.

All the backend has been implemented; we now need to develop some other resources in order to let our example function. Remember we specified some web pages in the classes up there? Well, that is what we will implement now.

The oauth-server project

As before, in order to create this project, you can use Maven commands or Eclipse IDE.

In order to turn this application, we must create the `jboss-web.xml` file with the following content:

```
<jboss-web>
    <security-domain>java:/jaas/commerce</security-domain>
    <valve>
        <class-name>org.jboss.resteasy.skeleton.key.as7.
OAuthAuthenticationServerValve</class-name>
    </valve>
</jboss-web>
```

One last thing: we have to create a JSON file with the purpose of having our certificates and security configuration in this server. We are going to name it `resteasy-oauth`. And as you can see, there is not a big deal with this file; it is a set of properties and values. Through this file, we specify the KeyStores and passwords, the truststore path, and so on. This file will be located in the `WEBINF` folder of this project.

```
{
  "realm" : "commerce",
```

```
      "admin-role" : "admin",
      "login-role" : "login",
      "oauth-client-role" : "oauth",
      "wildcard-role" : "*",
      "realm-keystore" : "${jboss.server.config.dir}/realm.jks",
      "realm-key-alias" : "commerce",
      "realm-keystore-password" : "changeit",
      "realm-private-key-password" : "changeit",
      "truststore" : "${jboss.server.config.dir}/client-truststore.ts",
      "truststore-password" : "changeit",
      "resources" : [
         "https://localhost:8443/oauth-client",
         "https://localhost:8443/discstore/"
      ]
  }
```

webapp/WEB-INF/ jboss-deployment-structure.xml

We must configure this file in all the projects because we updated some modules from the instance of JBoss AS. In this file, we must specify the dependencies our application has with some modules of JBoss. Then, we need to clearly set them using the `<module>` tag inside the `<dependencies>` tag, as follows:

```
<jboss-deployment-structure>
    <deployment>
        <!-- This allows you to define additional dependencies, it is
the same as using the Dependencies: manifest attribute -->
        <dependencies>
            <module name="org.jboss.resteasy.resteasy-jaxrs"
services="import"/>
            <module name="org.jboss.resteasy.resteasy-jackson-
provider" services="import"/>
            <module name="org.jboss.resteasy.skeleton-key" />
        </dependencies>
    </deployment>
</jboss-deployment-structure>
```

Running the application

We have explained the main parts of each project, so in order to run and test the application, you can download the examples folder of this chapter from `https://github.com/restful-java-web-services-security/source-code/tree/master/chapter04`. After you download the ZIP file, unzip it and you will find there is a folder named `OAuthExample`. Inside this folder, there are our three projects. You can copy them and paste them in your workspace and import the projects using Eclipse.

We have provided you the keystores, and certification and truststore files inside the `configuration` folder you just pasted while setting up the JBoss `configuration`. In order to make sure the application runs correctly, you may update these files, by following the instructions in the `.txt` file named `keystoreCommands` located inside the `configuration` folder.

In order to launch our application, we have to deploy it. So, open a terminal. Let's go to `JBOSS_HOME/bin` and start JBoss in standalone mode; this means executing `standalone.bat` if you are in Windows or `./standalone.sh` if you are in Linux. Then, open a terminal and go inside the folder of our application in the workspace. We have to execute the following commands: `mvn clean install` followed by `mvn jboss-as:deploy` on each one of the three projects that we have created: `discstore`, `oauth-client`, and `oauth-server`.

We have created a special class in the `discstore` project. This class contains a `void main` method, and we test our application through this class. We have named it `OAuthClientTest`. The code of this class is as follows:

```
public class OauthClientTest {

  public static void main(String[] args) throws Exception {

    String truststorePath =
      "C:/Users/Andres/jboss/2do_jboss/jboss-as-
      7.1.1.Final/standalone/configuration/client-truststore.ts";
    String truststorePassword = "changeit";
    truststorePath = EnvUtil.replace(truststorePath);

    KeyStore truststore = loadKeyStore(truststorePath,
      truststorePassword);

        ResteasyClient client = new ResteasyClientBuilder()
              .disableTrustManager().trustStore(truststore).build();

    Form form = new Form().param("grant_type",
      "client_credentials");
    ResteasyWebTarget target =
      client.target("https://localhost:8443/oauth-
      server/j_oauth_token_grant");
    target.register(new BasicAuthentication("andres", "andres"));

    AccessTokenResponse tokenResponse =
      target.request().post(Entity.form(form),
      AccessTokenResponse.class);
```

```
        Response response =
          client.target("https://localhost:8443/discstore/discs")
            .request()
            .header(HttpHeaders.AUTHORIZATION,
                "Bearer " + tokenResponse.getToken()).get();
      try {
        String xml = response.readEntity(String.class);
        System.out.println(xml);
      } finally {
        client.close();
      }

    }
```

We are going to explain the preceding code, first, we have two variables, `truststorePath` and `truststorePassword`. The first one is referencing the path of our `client-truststore.ts` file located in the configuration folder of our JBoss. You should change the value of this variable in order to make this test work, so place the path of your configuration folder. After this, with a method we already explained, `loadKeyStore ()`, we load the KeyStore using the previous variables and we assign this value to a `KeyStore` object named `truststore`. From `truststore`, we create the `RestEasyClient` object named `client`.

Now, we will obtain an access token programmatically, so we can request an access token from the auth-server simply by using HTTPS invocation. Then we have to use basic authentication to identify our user; as a result, we will get back a signed access token for that user.

So, we perform a simple POST to the context root of the auth-server with `j_oauth_token_grant` at the end of the target URL, because when we use that URL and a POST with basic authentication, we will obtain an access token for a specific user.

After that, we obtained the access token, which is a simple string. In order to invoke on a service protected by bearer token authentication, we have to build a string made up of the authorization header of your HTTPS request plus the string `Bearer` and finally the access token string. This will get back the response object, so we can read it and print it as we did in the test. In the console, you will see the list of compact discs as shown in the following screenshot:

SSO configuration for security management

SSO is a mechanism for authentication. It allows a user to access several systems or applications entering credentials just once. We think you experience this more often these days because we are living in a social network era, and most of these services let us use each other's credentials to access several services.

After discussing some concepts of SSO, let's try and implement this mechanism. In order to achieve this, we will use JBoss 7 Application Server and our earlier project `secure-demo`.

As a brief introduction to this implementation, we want to tell you that we will work with two files; one file belongs to JBoss and the other belongs to our application.

The file that belongs to JBoss is `standalone.xml`. We will add some lines to this file. In the following lines of code, let's add the SSO element in the `virtual-server` definition:

```
<subsystem xmlns="urn:jboss:domain:web:1.1" default-virtual-
server="default-host" native="false">
            <connector name="http" protocol="HTTP/1.1" scheme="http"
socket-binding="http"/>
            <virtual-server name="default-host" enable-welcome-
root="true">
```

```
            <alias name="localhost"/>
            <sso domain="localhost" reauthenticate="false"/>
        </virtual-server>
    </subsystem>
```

The `reauthenticate` attribute allows us to establish whether each request needs to be reauthenticated to `securityReal`. The default value is `false`.

The next file we must edit is in our application, and its name is `jboss-web.xml`. Also, we need to add some lines of code to this file. These lines of code will declare the valve that will manage the SSO. In other words, every request will go through this valve, as shown in the following code:

```
<jboss-web>
    <security-domain>java:/jaas/other </security-domain>
        <valve>
        <class-name>org.apache.catalina.authenticator.SingleSignOn</
class-name>
        </valve>
</jboss-web>
```

Just in case you forgot it or deleted it, we set a security domain in the previous chapters. The following block of code must exist in the `standalone.xml` file:

```
<security-domain name="other" cache-type="default">
    <authentication>
        <login-module code="Remoting" flag="optional">
<module-option name="password-stacking"  value="useFirstPass"/>
        </login-module>
        <login-module code="RealmUsersRoles" flag="required">
<module-option name="usersProperties" value="${jboss.server.config.
dir}/application-users.properties"/>
<module-option name="rolesProperties" value="${jboss.server.config.
dir}/application-roles.properties"/>
<module-option name="realm" value="ApplicationRealm"/>
<module-option name="password-stacking" value="useFirstPass"/>
        </login-module>
    </authentication>
</security-domain>
```

Since we are using the `secure-demo` example, this is all we must modify in order to configure SSO.

In order to test this mechanism, we need another application. We must replicate the configuration we just did in our `secure-demo` example.

When we enter the credentials in one of them, we no longer need to enter the credentials in the others, since we have applied SSO. We will authenticate in both applications.

OAuth token via Basic Auth

Now, let's explore and implement a short example of using tokens. In order to build this example, we will create a class. This class, as in the previous example, will simulate a database client. It will have the same method, `getCompactDiscs()`, but we will modify the internal function in this example. Also, it won't receive any parameter this time.

Alright, let's do it! First, create two static string fields in the class. The first field will hold the URL for authentication in the auth-server. The other field will have the URL showing the compact discs list; you can reuse the same web page from the previous example. Then, you should have your variables as shown:

```
private static String urlAuth = "https://localhost:8443/auth-server
/j_oauth_token_grant";
private static String urlDiscs = "https://localhost:8443/discstore/
discs";
```

After this, let's create our method to obtain the compact discs list. The following piece of code shows you exactly how the method is executed:

```
public static List<String> getCompactDiscs() {
  ResteasyClient rsClient = new ResteasyClientBuilder().
disableTrustManager().build();
    Form form = new Form().param("grant_type",
      "client_credentials");
  ResteasyWebTarget resourceTarget = rsClient.target(urlAuth);
    resourceTarget.register(new BasicAuthentication("andres",
"andres"));
  AccessTokenResponse accessToken = resourceTarget.request().
post(Entity.form(form), AccessTokenResponse.class);
    try {
      String bearerToken = "Bearer " + accessToken.getToken();
      Response response = rsClient.target(urlDiscs).request().
header(HttpHeaders.AUTHORIZATION, bearerToken).get();
      return response.readEntity(new GenericType<List<String>>() {
      });
    } finally {
      rsClient.close();
    }
  }
```

It is time to check what we have just done. As a first step, we created a `ResteasyClient` object. If you noticed, we used something to disable trust management and hostname verification. The result of this invocation is that it turns off server-certificate verification allowing MITM (man-in-the-middle) attacks. So, use this feature with caution.

After this, we create a `form` object and pass in some parameters. These parameters are passed in through the `param()` method, representing the parameter name and parameter value, respectively. This means we specify the type of grant being requested by the application, which will be `client_credentials`.

Then, as we did before in the previous example, let's create a RESTEasy web target that will target our URL showing the compact discs list. Remember that this URL was set in a static field we created earlier. This web target will be the `resourceTarget` object that we will access.

When we use the `register()` method and pass in a `BasicAuthentication` object, we register an instance of a custom JAX-RS component to be instantiated and used in the scope of this configurable context.

Moving forward, we create the `AccessTokenResponse` class by executing a request to our web target. Then, in the same line, we execute a post in order to send the entity and the response type we want to obtain for the current request synchronously. The `Entity.form()` method creates the `application/x-www-form-urlencoded` entity from the `form` object we created before. Now, this will return an `AccessTokenResponse` object; we use this object to build the bearer token by adding the word `Bearer` at the beginning of the token.

Finally, let's create the response object by executing a request to the URL that is set in the `urlDiscs` variable. We should use the `ResteasyClient` object to target this resource, and then execute the request and set the headers field with `HttpHeaders. AUTHORIZATION` using the `bearer` token set in the variable `bearerToken`. In this way, we gain access to the target resource; in this case, we can see the information.

As we keep using the same application business, we can reuse the web pages of the previous example. Make sure to incorporate in to your example, in the same path as in the previous example, the web pages `index.html` and `discsList.jsp`. We will also use the configuration set in the `jboss-deployment-structure.xml` file since we are using the same module dependencies.

Our `web.xml` file should look simpler than the previous example, so it might be something like the following:

```xml
<?xml version="1.0" encoding="UTF-8"?>
<web-app xmlns="http://java.sun.com/xml/ns/javaee"
```

```
      xmlns:xsi="http://www.w3.org/2001/XMLSchema-instance"
      xsi:schemaLocation="http://java.sun.com/xml/ns/javaee http://
   java.sun.com/xml/ns/javaee/web-app_3_0.xsd"
      version="3.0">
   <security-constraint>
      <web-resource-collection>
         <url-pattern>/*</url-pattern>
      </web-resource-collection>
      <user-data-constraint>
         <transport-guarantee>CONFIDENTIAL</transport-guarantee>
      </user-data-constraint>
   </security-constraint>
</web-app>
```

Running the application

You can download the complete code and configuration from `https://github.com/restful-java-web-services-security/source-code/tree/master/chapter04`. Unzip the file, and inside you will find a folder named `token-grant`. You have to deploy this project using the same commands. As a requirement, you have to deploy the projects `oauth-server`, `oauth-client`, and `discstore`.

It is time to run our application. Let's execute the steps we did in the previous example, the OAuth example. After this, we have to open our favorite browser and type the URL `https://localhost:8443/token-grant/`. This will lead us to the following web page:

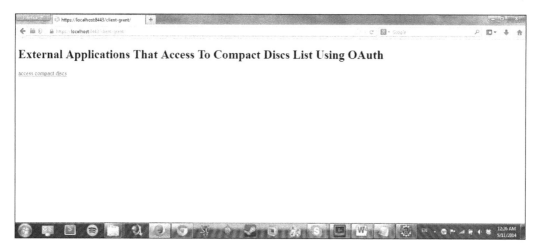

Well, as you notice, we reused the same web page, just for the purpose of these examples. There is, however, a little difference; when calling a different web page, you can look in the core we just explained. This will execute a token, where we will perform a request to the data we want to access through this token. As a result, we will read the list of our compact discs in the web page, as shown in the following screenshot:

The final result is the capability to present the discs list in the web page. However, don't forget what happened; we just obtained an access token response using the request, the basic authentication with our credentials, and a form. With the access token response, we can create the response and present the data with the respective authorization.

Custom filters

As a brief introduction, JAX-RS 2.0 has two different concepts for interceptions: filters and interceptors.

Interceptors are components that intercept EJB method invocations. They can be used to audit and log as and when EJBs are accessed. This is a topic that won't be included in this book, but if you feel curious and want to find out some more about it, we give you the following links as references so you can look it up:

- `http://docs.oracle.com/javaee/6/tutorial/doc/gkigq.html`
- `http://www.javacodegeeks.com/2013/07/java-ee-ejb-interceptors-tutorial-and-example.html`

Filters are mainly used to alter or process incoming and outgoing request or response headers. They can be executed before and after request and response processing.

Also, JAX-RS 2.0 offers us two categories of filters: server-side filters and client-side filters. The following diagram shows us a better classification of this concept:

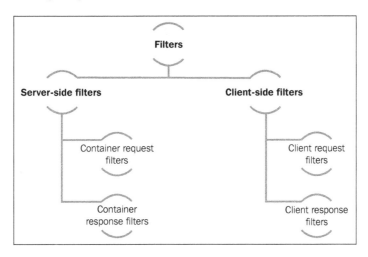

Server-side filters

When we are on the server side, we have another classification for these filters; container request filters are executed before the JAX-RS resource method is invoked. Also, we have the container response filters; you've probably guessed, they are executed after the JAX-RS resource method is invoked. However, this doesn't end here; there is another classification of container request filters: pre-matching and post-matching.

You can specify a pre-matching container request filter through the @PreMatching annotation, and this means that the filter will be executed before the JAX-RS resource method is matched with the incoming HTTP request.

Container request filters can abort the request by executing the abortWith (Response) method. A filter might want to abort if it implements a custom authentication protocol.

Once the resource class method has been executed, JAX-RS will run all container response filters. These filters let you modify the outgoing response before it is marshalled and is sent to the client.

Client-side filters

As we already told you, there are filters on the client side too, and similar to the server-side filters, they also have two types of filters: client request filters and client response filters. Client request filters are executed before your HTTP request is sent over the wire to the server. On the other hand, client response filters run after a response is received from the server, but before the response body is assembled.

Client request filters are also capable of aborting the request and providing a response without going over the wire to the server. Client response filters are capable of altering the response object before it is handed back to the application code.

Example usage of filters

After looking at some of the necessary theory around this topic, it is time to get your feet wet. Now, we will implement an example in order to support our new theoretical knowledge. So, let's start!

We will implement an interceptor that will verify the access permissions for a user, based on the username and password sent in the request. You can download the complete code of this example from the following link:

https://github.com/restful-java-web-services-security/source-code/ tree/master/chapter04

We have the topic of our compact discs store. So, the following class will represent our service, and it will have the functions to find the compact discs by name and update the compact disc information. The annotations used here have already been studied in the previous chapter, so you will probably find the following code understandable:

```
@Path("/compactDisc-service")
public class CompactDiscService {
  @PermitAll
  @GET
  @Path("/compactDiscs/{name}")
  public Response getCompactDiscByName(@PathParam("name") String name,
@Context Request request) {
    Response.ResponseBuilder rb =
      Response.ok(CompactDiscDatabase.getCompactDiscByName(name));
    return rb.build();
  }

  @RolesAllowed("ADMIN")
  @PUT
  @Path("/compactDiscs/{name}")
```

```
    public Response updatePriceByDiscName(@PathParam("name") String
name) {
      // Update the User resource
      CompactDiscDatabase.updateCompactDisc(name, 10.5);
      return Response.status(200).build();
    }
}
```

As you can see, we have created only two methods, one to retrieve compact discs by name and the other to update the compact discs' price. The annotations let us know that the method getCompactDiscByName() can be accessed and executed by all; meanwhile, the method updatePriceByDiscName() can be accessed and executed by users with the role ADMIN.

If you noticed in the preceding code, we used the class CompactDiscDatabase, which simulates a database. We applied the same technique in the previous examples. As it worked very well, let's do it again. This class doesn't have any special code. You can get an idea about this from the following code:

```
public class CompactDiscDatabase {
  public static HashMap<String, CompactDisc> compactDiscs = new
HashMap<String, CompactDisc>();

  static {
    CompactDisc ramonesCD = new CompactDisc();
    ramonesCD.setDiscName("Ramones Anthology");
    ramonesCD.setBandName("The Ramones");
    ramonesCD.setPrice(15.0);

    Calendar calendar = Calendar.getInstance();
    calendar.set(1980, 10, 22);
    Date realeaseDate = calendar.getTime();
    ramonesCD.setReleaseDate(realeaseDate);
    compactDiscs.put("Ramones Anthology", ramonesCD);

  }

  public static CompactDisc getCompactDiscByName(String name) {
    return compactDiscs.get(name);
  }

  public static void updateCompactDisc(String name, double newPrice) {
    CompactDisc cd = compactDiscs.get(name);
    cd.setPrice(newPrice);
  }
}
```

There is nothing complex here; we just created a map and put one entry there. This entry is a compact disc object, as you can tell. We have two static methods that will simulate queries—a SELECT statement and an UPDATE statement.

Now, let's check our `CompactDisc` class, as shown in the following code:

```
@XmlAccessorType(XmlAccessType.NONE)
@XmlRootElement(name = "compactDisc")
public class CompactDisc implements Serializable {
    private static final long serialVersionUID = 1L;

    @XmlElement(name = "discName")
    private String discName;

    @XmlElement(name = "bandName")
    private String bandName;

    @XmlElement(name = "releaseDate")
    private Date releaseDate;

    @XmlElement(name = "price")
    private double price;
//getters and setters
}
```

In this class, we just set the fields that represent a common compact disc attribute. The annotation `@XmlElement` is used to map a property to an XML element derived from a property name.

Now, it is time to implement the filter. We will show you the code after this short introduction, explain what we have done, and explain some technical concepts used in the implementation. Ready? Here we go!

Since the code of this class is a little bit long, we will split it and include a short description after each block of code, as follows:

```
@Provider
public class SecurityFilter implements javax.ws.rs.container.
ContainerRequestFilter {

    private static final String ADMIN = "ADMIN";
    private static final String RESOURCE_METHOD_INVOKER = "org.jboss.
resteasy.core.ResourceMethodInvoker";
    private static final String AUTHORIZATION_PROPERTY =
"Authorization";
    private static final String AUTHENTICATION_SCHEME = "Basic";
    private static final ServerResponse ACCESS_DENIED = new
ServerResponse("Access denied for this resource", 401,
        new Headers<Object>());
```

```
    private static final ServerResponse ACCESS_FORBIDDEN = new
ServerResponse("Nobody can access this resource", 403,
    new Headers<Object>());
```

Let's check out this code. The first step, in order to implement a filter, is the annotation @Provider. When we place this annotation at class level, we set the class as a filter. Our class name is SecurityFilter, and as you can see, it implements the interface ContainerRequestFilter. If you remember, this filter will execute on the server side and before the resource method is invoked.

At the start of our class's body, we set some constants that we will use later. The AUTHORIZATION_PROPERTY constant represents just the name of a property, as does the RESOURCE_METHOD_INVOKER constant. The AUTHENTICATION_SCHEME constant represents just a string. Both ACCESS_DENIED and ACCESS_FORBIDDEN constants represent two different server response objects in order to notify the user of the result of their request when it is denied or the user doesn't have enough permission.

As we implemented the interface ContainerRequestFilter, we must override the filter() method. It is inside this method that we will put our logic for the purpose of filtering the request based on the user that executed the request.

Let's start. As a first step, we obtain the method of the request using the constant RESOURCE_METHOD_INVOKER. After this, we will have a ResourceMethodInvoker object, and then the Method object, as shown in the following code:

```
@Override
public void filter(ContainerRequestContext requestContext) {
    ResourceMethodInvoker methodInvoker = (ResourceMethodInvoker)
      requestContext
        .getProperty(RESOURCE_METHOD_INVOKER);
    Method method = methodInvoker.getMethod();
```

Next, we will perform some simple validations over method. We will check whether the method is annotated with @PermitAll. If it isn't, then the method continues, and we check whether it is annotated with @DenyAll. If the method is annotated with DenyAll, then we abort the request, including the constant ACCESS_FORBIDDEN, as shown in the following code:

```
// Access allowed for all
    if (!method.isAnnotationPresent(PermitAll.class)) {
        // Access denied for all
        if (method.isAnnotationPresent(DenyAll.class)) {
          requestContext.abortWith(ACCESS_FORBIDDEN);
          return;
        }
```

Now, we have to obtain the username and password. We must first obtain the headers of the request and put it in a map. Then, we obtain the authorization string list using `constant AUTHORIZATION_PROPERTY` as a key. This list will let us know whether the user has enough permission or not. So, we check if the list is empty or null; if it enters the `if()` block, we abort the request, including the constant `ACCESS_DENIED`, as shown in the following code:

```
final MultivaluedMap<String, String> headersMap =
  requestContext.getHeaders();

final List<String> authorizationList =
  headersMap.get(AUTHORIZATION_PROPERTY);

if (authorizationList == null ||
  authorizationList.isEmpty()) {
  requestContext.abortWith(ACCESS_DENIED);
  return;
}
```

This list has the encoded username and password as a string in the first element. So, we execute a replacement and eliminate the string contained in the constant `AUTHENTICATION_SCHEME`. Then, we decode it using the `Base64.decodeBase64` decoder, and through `StringTokenizer`, we obtain the username and password separated. Let's look at the following code:

```
final String encodedUserPassword =
  authorizationList.get(0).replaceFirst(AUTHENTICATION_SCHEME +
  " ", "");

String usernameAndPassword = new
  String(Base64.decodeBase64(encodedUserPassword));

// Split username and password tokens
final StringTokenizer tokenizer = new
  StringTokenizer(usernameAndPassword, ":");
final String userName = tokenizer.nextToken();
final String password = tokenizer.nextToken();
```

Now is the time to evaluate and check whether the user has enough permission. First, let's check whether `method` has the `@RolesAllowed` annotation; if it does, we obtain the set of roles allowed using the object `method`. Finally, we check whether the constant `ADMIN` is included in this list. If it is not, the request is aborted and `ACCESS_DENIED` is once again included, as shown in the following code:

```
      // Verify user access
    if (method.isAnnotationPresent(RolesAllowed.class)) {
      RolesAllowed rolesAnnotation = method.
       getAnnotation(RolesAllowed.class);
      Set<String> rolesSet = new HashSet<String>(Arrays.
 asList(rolesAnnotation.value()));

      // Is user valid?
      if (!isUserAllowed(userName, password, rolesSet)) {
      requestContext.abortWith(ACCESS_DENIED);
        return;
      }
    }
   }
  }



  private boolean isUserAllowed(final String username, final
    String password, final Set<String> rolesSet) {
    boolean isAllowed = false;

    if (rolesSet.contains(ADMIN)) {
      isAllowed = true;
    }
    return isAllowed;
  }
}
```

Summary

In this chapter, we studied and implemented one of the most useful and necessary techniques with the purpose of sharing and protecting our information. Nowadays, applications have dramatically increased their interaction with each other because they want to meet and satisfy the requirements of clients, users, and so on, compromising neither the security nor the integrity of the data while doing this.

In this chapter, we studied several technologies to secure, limit, and authorize the use of our resources to a third-party application, starting with brief but descriptive concepts about OAuth 2.0 authentication, Single Sign-On, filters, and tokens.

Through a practical example and real code, you witnessed how you can grant permission over specific resources to a third-party application in order to share the information and maintain control over it. Also, we checked and worked with specific code to implement one of the most used technologies in recent times, especially in the world of social networks, Single Sign-On. Now, you can put in to practice these concepts and technologies in order to build applications to interact with each other, selecting which resource you want to be shared, which applications you want to use as Single Sign-On, and filtering the use of certain resources based on the user and role.

5
Digital Signatures and Encryption of Messages

Since many systems interact with each other to achieve their business goals, we often feel the obligation to interact with services exposed by others. Also, when security needs play an important role, we must verify that the information we receive has been sent from whom we expected, and it has come without being altered. It is here where digital signatures will play an important role and help us meet this need.

Also, we may sometimes need to encrypt the message body to prevent it from being read if intercepted by unwanted persons. It is here where we can make use of Secure/Multipurpose Internet Mail Extensions, or the S/MIME standard, which is commonly used in the world of e-mail for public keys (`http://en.wikipedia.org/wiki/Public_key`), encryption (`http://en.wikipedia.org/wiki/Encryption`), and signing (`http://en.wikipedia.org/wiki/Digital_signature`) of MIME data (`http://en.wikipedia.org/wiki/MIME`), and which also offers the ability to adapt the HTTP protocol and allows us to use it on RESTful web services.

In this chapter, we are going to learn about the following:

* Signing messages
* Verifying signatures
* Encrypting message bodies with S/MIME

Digital signatures

Digital signatures, nowadays, are a widely used mechanism. They are mainly used to sign digital documents and issue electronic invoices, among other things.

Among the benefits of using them are the following:

- They allow the receiver to obtain the identity of whoever has made the signature.
- They provide the ability to verify that the information sent has not been altered since it has been signed by the issuer.

In order to electronically sign the information that we will exchange through RESTful web services, we will use the authentication mechanism known as **DomainKeys Identified Mail (DKIM)**, which allows us to decorate messages with headers using the rules dictated by the DOSETA specification. This authentication mechanism is mainly used for e-mail identity verification; however, it also works over other protocols such as HTTP, and it is because of this fact we can integrate it with RESTful web services. Thus, we will inject metadata into our messages with the purpose of signing, and these signatures can be verified by those who wish to consume.

At this time, we will build an example that shows how to sign a message, and then dissect each part of it to understand its operation.

If you want, you can download the source code using the following link on GitHub:

```
https://github.com/restful-java-web-services-security/source-code/
tree/master/chapter05/signatures
```

Otherwise, we will explain it in the following pages. Let's start by creating a new project. Open the terminal and type the following:

```
mvn archetype:generate -DgroupId=com.packtpub -DartifactId=signatures
  -DarchetypeArtifactId=webapp-javaee6 -
  DarchetypeGroupId=org.codehaus.mojo.archetypes
```

When it asks you for the version, change the default value 1.0-SNAPSHOT to 1.0

Now, we will generate the keys that allow us to encrypt messages and place them in the classpath of our application. For this, we will first import the project into Eclipse IDE and then create a folder within the project in which we place the keys that we want to generate. In Eclipse, right-click on the new project named signatures and select the option **New | Source folder**.

In the field **Folder name**, we will enter `src/main/resources`, and then we press the **Finish** button.

Now, let's go to this directory from the command line and execute the following instruction:

```
keytool -genkeypair -alias demo._domainKey.packtpub.com -keyalg RSA
-keysize 1024 -keystore demo.jks
```

Now, we should enter a password for both the KeyStore and the keys with which we will sign the message. When it asks you for a password, type `changeit`, which is the same password we have been using so far in our examples in this book. Then, we enter the requested information as shown in the following screenshot:

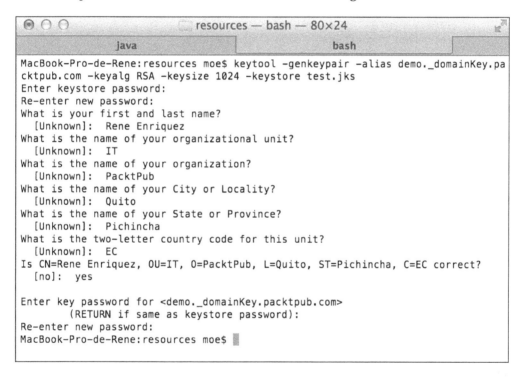

Now, we will implement some source code to sign a message. We first need to add the required dependencies to the `pom.xml` file.

First, add the JBoss repository from which we get the artifacts, as shown in the following code:

```
<repositories>
  <repository>
    <id>jboss</id>
    <url>http://repository.jboss.org/maven2</url>
  </repository>
</repositories>
```

Now, let's add all the dependencies we need to sign our message, as follows:

```
<dependencies>
  <dependency>
    <groupId>org.jboss.resteasy</groupId>
    <artifactId>resteasy-jaxrs</artifactId>
    <version>3.0.6.Final</version>
  </dependency>
  <dependency>
    <groupId>org.jboss.resteasy</groupId>
    <artifactId>resteasy-crypto</artifactId>
    <version>3.0.6.Final</version>
  </dependency>
</dependencies>
```

With the purpose of avoiding duplicated classes in the classpath, we should delete the following dependency:

```
<dependency>
  <groupId>javax</groupId>
  <artifactId>javaee-web-api</artifactId>
  <version>6.0</version>
  <scope>provided</scope>
</dependency>
```

Updating RESTEasy JAR files

As we are using the 3.0.6.Final Version to compile the project, it is necessary to update the existing versions in JBoss. So, we will go to the URL `http://sourceforge.net/projects/resteasy/files/Resteasy%20JAX-RS/` and download the version we just described.

When we unzip the `.zip` file, we will find a file named `resteasy-jboss-modules-3.0.6.Final.zip`. Let's unzip this file too, and then paste all its content in our directory `JBOSS_HOME/modules`. Given RESTEasy modules have dependencies, we have to update them too. So, after we update the RESTEasy modules, we should update the module `org.apache.httpcomponents`. Let's go to the directory `JBOSS_HOME/modules/org/apache/httpcomponents` and update the following artifacts:

- `httpclient-4.1.2.jar` to `httpclient-4.2.1.jar`
- `httpcore-4.1.4.jar` to `httpcore-4.2.1.jar`

Also, we modify the `module.xml` file because the names of the JAR files are different, as follows:

```xml
<?xml version="1.0" encoding="UTF-8"?>

<!--
 ...
  -->

<module xmlns="urn:jboss:module:1.1" name="org.apache.httpcomponents">
    <properties>
        <property name="jboss.api" value="private"/>
    </properties>

    <resources>
        <resource-root path="httpclient-4.2.1.jar"/>
        <resource-root path="httpcore-4.2.1.jar"/>
        <resource-root path="httpmime-4.1.2.jar"/>
        <!-- Insert resources here -->
    </resources>

    <dependencies>
        <module name="javax.api"/>
        <module name="org.apache.commons.codec"/>
        <module name="org.apache.commons.logging"/>
        <module name="org.apache.james.mime4j"/>
    </dependencies>
</module>
```

Applying digital signatures

Now that we have everything we need to compile our project, we will create a very simple operation and apply a signature. In order to achieve this, let's create a class called `SignedService` in the source code package called `com.packtpub.resteasy.services`, as shown in the following screenshot:

To sign a message, we take a key from the KeyStore and use it. We can identify the keys in a unique way through their alias and the domain they belong to. For example, for the key demo._domainKey.packtpub.com, the alias is demo and the domain it belongs to is the key packtpub.com. Given that we can find several keys in a KeyStore, RESTEasy offers the capability to select the one we want by using the annotation @Signed.

Let's add the method highlighted in the following code to the class and watch how the annotation works:

```
@POST
@Produces("text/plain")
@Signed(selector = "demo", domain = "packtpub.com")
public String sign(String input) {
  System.out.println("Aplyng signature " + input);
  return "signed " + input;
}
```

The following figure shows us in a better way how the key is selected to sign the message:

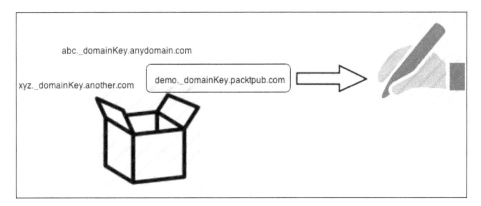

Now, we will define the path under our signed resources will be available, so let's annotate the class as follows:

```
import javax.ws.rs.Consumes;
import javax.ws.rs.POST;
import javax.ws.rs.Path;

import org.jboss.resteasy.annotations.security.doseta.Signed;

@Path("/signed")
public class SignedService {
  ...
```

In order to make the application work properly, we will give it information so that it can apply the appropriate signatures.

First, in the folder `src/main/webapp`, we will create the `WEB-INF` folder with an empty `web.xml` file inside.

Let's start with the `web.xml` file, which should look like the following:

```
<?xml version="1.0" encoding="UTF-8"?>
<web-app version="3.0" xmlns="http://java.sun.com/xml/ns/javaee"
    xmlns:xsi="http://www.w3.org/2001/XMLSchema-instance"
    xsi:schemaLocation="http://java.sun.com/xml/ns/javaee
    http://java.sun.com/xml/ns/javaee/web-app_3_0.xsd">

    <display-name>signatures</display-name>

</web-app>
```

Now, the first thing we will do is tell our application what resource we want to sign, which is the class that contains the method that we are signing. For this, let's configure the parameter `resteasy.resources` with the corresponding full class name, as follows:

```
<context-param>
<param-name>resteasy.resources</param-name>
<param-value>com.packtpub.resteasy.services.SignedResource</param-value>
</context-param>
```

Next, we will inform our application of the location of the key with which we apply the signature (the `.jks` file we created earlier). For this, we have two context parameters available, `resteasy.doseta.keystore.classpath` and `resteasy.keystore.filename`. Let's use the first parameter so that our file looks like the following:

```
<context-param>
<param-name>resteasy.doseta.keystore.classpath</param-name>
<param-value>demo.jks</param-value>
</context-param>
```

As you remember, we were asked for a password for the KeyStore when creating the key. We will tell our application what this is using the parameter `resteasy.doseta.keystore.password`. Let's add the following content:

```
<context-param>
    <param-name>resteasy.doseta.keystore.password</param-name>
    <param-value>changeit</param-value>
</context-param>
```

To create the KeyStore from which we will extract the key that will allow us to sign the message, we must add the following parameter:

```
<context-param>
  <param-name>resteasy.context.objects</param-name>
  <param-value>org.jboss.resteasy.security.doseta.KeyRepository :
    org.jboss.resteasy.security.doseta.ConfiguredDosetaKey
    Repository</param-value>
</context-param>
```

Finally, we should add the RESTEasy servlet, as follows:

```
<servlet>
  <servlet-name>Resteasy</servlet-name>
  <servlet-class>org.jboss.resteasy.plugins.server.servlet.
HttpServlet
Dispatcher</servlet-class>
</servlet>
<servlet-mapping>
  <servlet-name>Resteasy</servlet-name>
  <url-pattern>/*</url-pattern>
</servlet-mapping>
```

Here, we show how the `web.xml` file should look once you have finished adding all the required information:

```
<?xml version="1.0" encoding="UTF-8"?>
<web-app version="3.0" xmlns="http://java.sun.com/xml/ns/javaee"
  xmlns:xsi="http://www.w3.org/2001/XMLSchema-instance"
  xsi:schemaLocation="http://java.sun.com/xml/ns/javaee
  http://java.sun.com/xml/ns/javaee/web-app_3_0.xsd">
<web-app>
  <display-name>signatures</display-name>
  <context-param>
    <param-name>resteasy.resources</param-name>
    <param-value>com.packtpub.resteasy.services.Signed
      Service</param-value>
  </context-param>
  <context-param>
    <param-name>resteasy.doseta.keystore.classpath</param-name>
    <param-value>demo.jks</param-value>
  </context-param>
  <context-param>
    <param-name>resteasy.doseta.keystore.password</param-name>
    <param-value>changeit</param-value>
  </context-param>
  <context-param>
```

```
            <param-name>resteasy.context.objects</param-name>
            <param-value>org.jboss.resteasy.security.doseta.Key
Repository : org.jboss.resteasy.security.doseta.ConfiguredDosetaKey
Repository</param-value>
        </context-param>
        <servlet>
            <servlet-name>Resteasy</servlet-name>
            <servlet-class>org.jboss.resteasy.plugins.server.servlet.
HttpServlet
Dispatcher</servlet-class>
        </servlet>
        <servlet-mapping>
            <servlet-name>Resteasy</servlet-name>
            <url-pattern>/*</url-pattern>
        </servlet-mapping>
    </web-app>
```

Now, let's generate the WAR file by executing the following command:

```
mvn install
```

After this, we will copy the generated artifact in to the JBoss deploy directory.

Testing the functionality

Now, open SoapUI and test whether the web service is running as expected, as shown in the following screenshot:

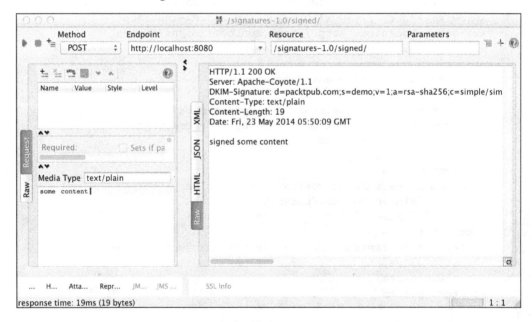

As you can see in the response, we obtain the DKIM-Signature header used to sign the message. The full content of this header is as follows:

```
DKIM-Signature: d=packtpub.com;s=demo;v=1;a=rsa-sha256;c=simple/simple
;bh=lc+ECoAqpQCB4ItWLUomBv34m3F9G0pkIBAI8Z/yWcQ=;b=AlJY6iiCtdCnHrJa+Of
9aRgBXeIp7V7cEG7eyUp0CRbD9wjFodbQGRQjhfwDgd1WIBzVLIWelTdI85BlGl3ACNcML
BjPv2iBBjo+78e/9HcYs81YNlPRAAj6jzymA/+jkmpTVcthWaEEyoPJJBAI5FvP33zH7e
tfkFaGX+bwer0=
```

From this whole string, what is important for us are the following:

- d=: This is the domain, the value which is indicated at the time we implement the method.
- a=: This is the algorithm used by RESTEasy to sign the message. In this case, we use RSA because it is the only algorithm that is supported to date by the framework.

The other parameters are not very important, and they are only necessary for a signed message.

Now, in order to validate the authenticity of the signature, we will create a class from which we will make the verification.

We will use JUnit; so, first add the corresponding dependency in the pom.xml file, as shown in the following code snippet:

```
<dependency>
  <groupId>junit</groupId>
  <artifactId>junit</artifactId>
  <version>4.8.2</version>
  <scope>test</scope>
</dependency>
```

Now, let's create a new source folder named scr/test/java and a package named com.packtpub.resteasy.services.test inside it. Inside the package, let's create the class SignedServiceTest using the following content:

```
import javax.ws.rs.client.Entity;
import javax.ws.rs.client.Invocation;
import javax.ws.rs.client.WebTarget;
import javax.ws.rs.core.Response;
import junit.framework.Assert;
import org.jboss.resteasy.client.jaxrs.ResteasyClient;
import org.jboss.resteasy.client.jaxrs.ResteasyClientBuilder;
import org.jboss.resteasy.security.doseta.DosetaKeyRepository;
import org.jboss.resteasy.security.doseta.Verification;
import org.jboss.resteasy.security.doseta.Verifier;
```

```
import org.junit.Test;

public class SignedServiceTest {

  @Test
  public void testVerification() {
    // Keys repository
    DosetaKeyRepository repository = new DosetaKeyRepository();
    repository.setKeyStorePath("demo.jks");
    repository.setKeyStorePassword("changeit");
    repository.start();
    // Building the client
  ResteasyClient client = new ResteasyClientBuilder().build();
    Verifier verifier = new Verifier();
    Verification verification = verifier.addNew();
    verification.setRepository(repository);
    WebTarget target = client
            .target(
      "http://localhost:8080/signatures-1.0/signed");
    Invocation.Builder request = target.request();
    request.property(Verifier.class.getName(), verifier);
    // Invocation to RESTful web service
    Response response = request.post(Entity.text("Rene"));
    // Status 200 OK
    Assert.assertEquals(200, response.getStatus());
    System.out.println(response.readEntity(String.class));
    response.close();
    client.close();
  }
}
```

If everything goes well, we will see a green bar as a result of our test, as shown in the following screenshot:

Validating signatures with annotations

A simpler way to validate whether a resource is signed is to use annotations. This solution can be used mainly when you have a flow of signatures that must be met.

For example, imagine that employees of the company Packt Publishing have a system through which they can apply to increase the RAM of their computers. To treat such requests as valid, they must be signed by the person making the request. We mean that we only need that the request be signed to be considered valid, as shown in the following figure:

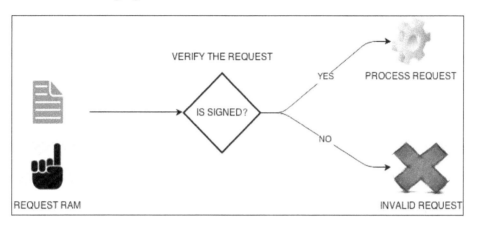

For this example, we will add two methods to our `SignedService` class; the first method will allow us to send the requests, as shown:

```
@POST
@Path("ram")
@Signed(selector = "demo", domain = "packtpub.com")
@Consumes("text/plain")
public String requestRam(int numberOfGB) {
  return numberOfGB + "-GB";
}
```

To meet the business requirements, we will use the `@Verify` annotation in which we can add restrictions on signatures. For now, we only need to verify that the request is signed.

The following is the method that shows all the complicated logic used by the boss to approve or deny memory increases to employee PCs:

```
@Verify
@POST
@Path("verifier")
```

```
@Produces("text/plain")
public String processRequestRam (String input) {
    int numberOfGbRequested = Integer.valueOf(input.split("-")[0]);
    if (numberOfGbRequested > 4) {
        return "deny";
    } else {
        return "accepted";
    }
}
```

Now, let's deploy the application on JBoss and test it with SoapUI. As we have mentioned, the requests must be signed in order to be processed. So, first make a request to the method `processRequestRam` without a signature, as shown in the following screenshot:

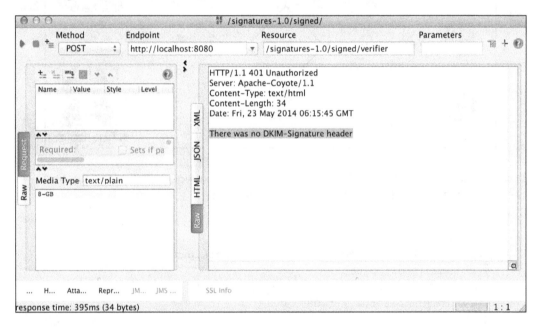

What is essential for the application to be processed is that it comes from the company domain, in this case, `packtpub.com`. Later, the boss conducts a rigorous analysis of the application and issues a judgment to determine whether the application is approved or rejected.

For this example, we will remove the method that we created earlier and add two methods to our `SignedService` class; the first method will allow us to send the requests, as shown:

```
@POST
@Signed(selector = "demo", domain = "packtpub.com")
@Consumes("text/plain")
public Response requestRAM(int numberOfGB) {
  return Response.seeOther(
    URI.create("/signed/" + "GB:" + numberOfGB)).build();
}
```

The output shows us the error very clearly. The request couldn't be processed because there is no `DKIM-Signature` header that contains the information to verify the signature. This means that the headers aren't there because they weren't signed earlier.

In order to get the request successfully processed, we will call a web service that signs the request. We will add the headers with the signature information and call the `processRequestRam` method again.

Let' start by calling the `requestRam` operation, as shown in the following screenshot:

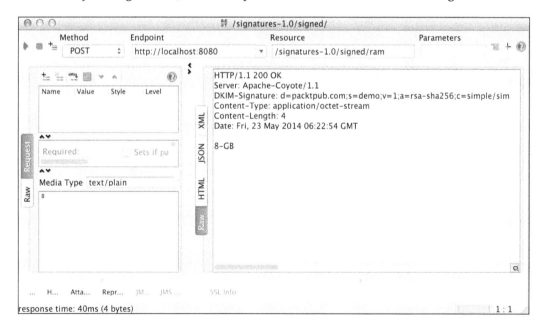

As a result of this callback, we will obtain the following values:

```
DKIM-Signature: d=packtpub.com;s=demo;v=1;a=rsa-sha256;c=simple/simple
;bh=uA6n2udZlWdx+ouwCEeeyM6Q48KH0EWa2MnfBwMP+vM=;b=T0drw9QWud7rs1w//53
84hs8GCatJKzmljIhgiTrHWdVx/IhCVl915yycchN+hQ+ljUaS6bPtLYo/ZNspcv2LtAe/
tKTPpng4RWlr52k0TqnV3XX2KvJ7kBOpEU2Rg6f6lBOJT5v+o0iV05ObagfzKDfQ9o09W
pZjQKcBG+/xvE=


RESPONSE: 8 GB
```

Let's keep moving! Now, we will use these values to make a request. From SoapUI, let's invoke the `processRequestRam` operation and focus on the bottom-left area of our request editor; there is an option that says **Header**. Let's select this option and click on the + symbol. Now, we have to enter the `DKIM-Signature` header and place the corresponding value. Also, don't forget to send the request parameter `8-GB` that was the response of the invocation of the `requestRam` operation, as highlighted in the following screenshot:

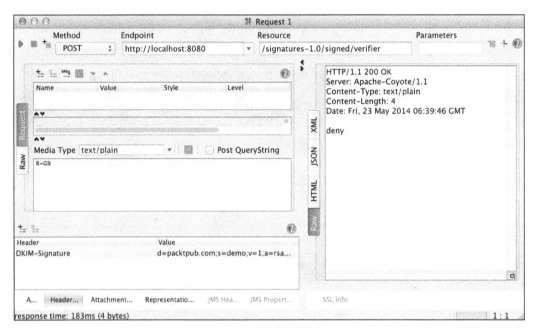

As we can see, the request was successfully processed, but the boss denied the increase of memory. Now, we indicate that digital signatures allow us to validate that the information is not altered once it has been signed. Suppose malicious software intercepted the response, and instead of 8-GB, it delivered the value 12-GB. Let's make this request in SoapUI following the theory of digital signatures. This request should not be valid; however, we must check:

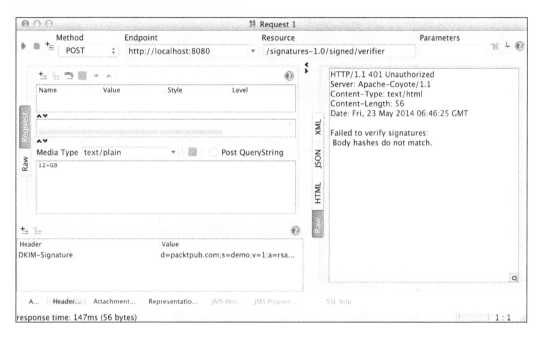

The error message clearly indicates that the message body was altered, so the request is not processed and we get the HTTP 401 Unauthorized message. This corroborates the statement made before regarding the integrity of the signed messages.

RESTEasy allows us, however, to do more than just validate that a message has been signed. We can verify that the signer belongs to a specific domain. In our example, a firm would be considered valid only when it comes under the `packtpub.com` domain. To perform this type of control, we will make the following change:

```java
@Verify(identifierName = "d", identifierValue = "packtpub.com")
@POST
@Path("verifier")
@Produces("text/plain")
public String processRequestRam(String input) {
   int numberOfGbRequested = Integer.valueOf(input.split("-")[0]);
   if (numberOfGbRequested > 4) {
     return "deny";
   } else {
     return "accepted";
   }
}
```

Let's deploy the application in JBoss and execute the request again from SoapUI:

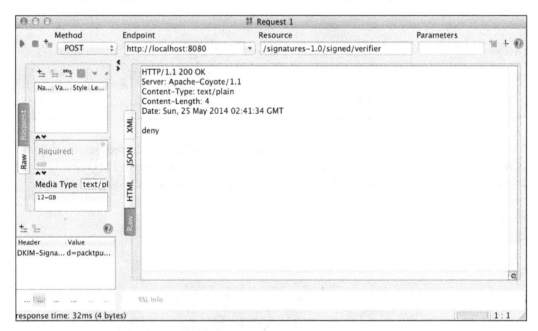

Now, let's force a fault. We will assume that valid messages are only those that are signed from the domain `itpacktpub.com`. So, let's apply the following change:

```java
@Verify(identifierName = "d", identifierValue = "itpacktpub.com")
@POST
@Path("verifier")
@Produces("text/plain")
public String processRequestRam(String input) {
    int numberOfGbRequested = Integer.valueOf(input.split("-")[0]);
    if (numberOfGbRequested > 4) {
        return "deny";
    } else {
        return "accepted";
    }
}
```

Let's deploy the application in JBoss again, and execute the request from SoapUI:

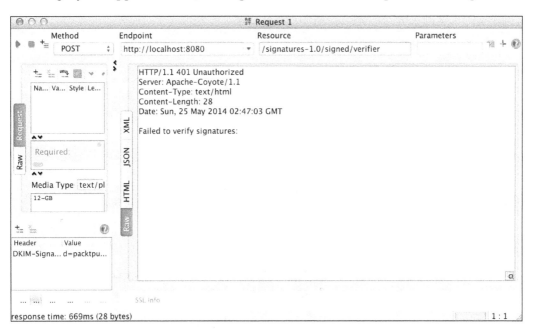

As we expected, the request failed this time. Obviously, this happened because the signatures could not be verified as the message was signed with the `packtpub.com` domain and not with the `itpacktpub.com` domain as we set in the operation `processRequestRam`.

Suddenly, you wonder why the value of the identified name is d. As we mentioned before, the letter d represents the domain. The RESTEasy documentation explains a little more about each of the parameters in the header. Here, we show you an example from the documentation about JBoss related to this topic:

Here's what an example DKIM-Signature header might look like:

DKIM-Signature: v=1;

> *a=rsa-sha256;*

> *d=example.com;*

> *s=burke;*

> *c=simple/simple;*

> *h=Content-Type;*

> *x=0023423111111;*

> *bh=2342322111;*

> *b=M232234=*

As you can see, it is a set of name value pairs delimited by a ';'. While it's not THAT important to know the structure of the header, here's an explanation of each parameter:

v: Protocol version. Always 1.

a: Algorithm used to hash and sign the message. RSA signing and SHA256 hashing is the only supported algorithm at the moment by RESTEasy.

d: Domain of the signer. This is used to identify the signer as well as discover the public key to use to verify the signature.

s: Selector of the domain. Also used to identify the signer and discover the public key.

c: Canonical algorithm. Only simple/simple is supported at the moment. Basically, this allows you to transform the message body before calculating the hash.

h: Semi-colon delimited list of headers that are included in the signature calculation.

x: When the signature expires. This is a numeric long value of the time in seconds since epoch. Allows signer to control when a signed message's signature expires.

t: Timestamp of signature. Numeric long value of the time in seconds since epoch. Allows the verifier to control when a signature expires.

bh: Base 64 encoded hash of the message body.

b: Base 64 encoded signature.

Now that we have this information, it is clear to assume that if you want to check the signer, instead of using the letter d, we must use the letter s, and instead of packtpub.com, we will use demo. Once you apply these changes, our code should look like the following:

```
@Verify(identifierName = "s", identifierValue = "demo")
@POST
@Path("verifier")
@Produces("text/plain")
public String processRequestRam(String input) {
  int numberOfGbRequested = Integer.valueOf(input.split("-")[0]);
  if (numberOfGbRequested > 4) {
    return "deny";
  } else {
    return "accepted";
  }
}
```

In addition, if you want to verify the signer's name and domain, you must apply a slight change. This time, we will use the @Verifications annotation; this annotation receives an array of @Verify annotations as a parameter, which allows us to perform what we described earlier. In this case, we should add two controls using the @Verify annotation, and our code should look like the following:

```
@Verifications({
@Verify(identifierName = "s", identifierValue = "demo"),
@Verify(identifierName = "d", identifierValue = "packtpub.com") })
@POST
@Path("verifier")
@Produces("text/plain")
public String processRequestRam(String input) {
  int numberOfGbRequested = Integer.valueOf(input.split("-")[0]);
  if (numberOfGbRequested > 4) {
```

```
        return "deny";
    } else {
        return "accepted";
    }
}
```

Once we have applied the changes, we can perform a request using SoapUI. We should get a successful execution as the result, as shown in the following screenshot:

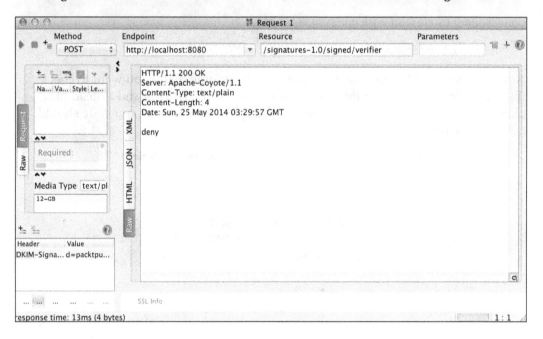

Message body encryption

In the previous chapter, we saw how to encrypt a complete HTTP message using HTTPS. Now, we will explain how we can encrypt just the message body and the differences between each process. We start by constructing a simple example, and then, as we perform the respective tests of our implementation, we'll understand how it works.

In order not to spoil our previous project, we will build a new one. For this, we will execute the following commands in the terminal:

```
mvn archetype:generate -DgroupId=com.packtpub -DartifactId=encryption
-DarchetypeArtifactId=webapp-javaee6 -DarchetypeGroupId=org.codehaus.
mojo.archetypes
```

As seen earlier in this chapter, when you get asked for a version, change the default value of 1.0-SNAPSHOT to 1.0.

Of course, if you want, you can download all the source code from GitHub from the following URL:

https://github.com/restful-java-web-services-security/source-code/
tree/master/chapter05/encryption

Now, let's import the project into Eclipse, delete the existing default dependence in the pom.xml file, and add dependencies on the artifacts resteasy-jaxrs and resteasy-crypto.

The dependencies section should look like the following:

```
<dependencies>
  <dependency>
    <groupId>org.jboss.resteasy</groupId>
    <artifactId>resteasy-jaxrs</artifactId>
    <version>3.0.6.Final</version>
    <scope>provided</scope>
  </dependency>
  <dependency>
    <groupId>org.jboss.resteasy</groupId>
    <artifactId>resteasy-crypto</artifactId>
    <version>3.0.6.Final</version>
  </dependency>
</dependencies>
```

Now, let's create the class EncryptedService inside the package com.packtpub. In this class, we will create a very simple operation, as shown:

```
package com.packtpub;

import javax.ws.rs.GET;
import javax.ws.rs.Path;

@Path("/encrypted")
public class EncryptedService {

  @GET
  public String gretting() {
    return "Hello world";
  }
}
```

To register the services of our application, let's create the class
EncryptedApplication, as shown:

```
package com.packtpub;

import java.util.HashSet;
import java.util.Set;

import javax.ws.rs.ApplicationPath;
import javax.ws.rs.core.Application;

@ApplicationPath("/services")
public class EncryptedApplication extends Application {

  private Set<Object> resources = new HashSet<Object>();

  public EncryptedApplication() throws Exception {
    resources.add(new EncryptedService());
  }

  @Override
  public Set<Object> getSingletons() {
    return resources;
  }
}
```

Testing the functionality

After this, our application should be ready. So, let's execute a test from SoapUI to
watch the traffic using Wireshark, as shown in the following screenshot:

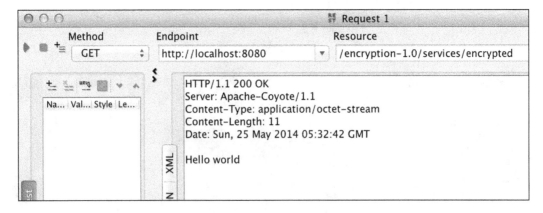

Wireshark shows us the following:

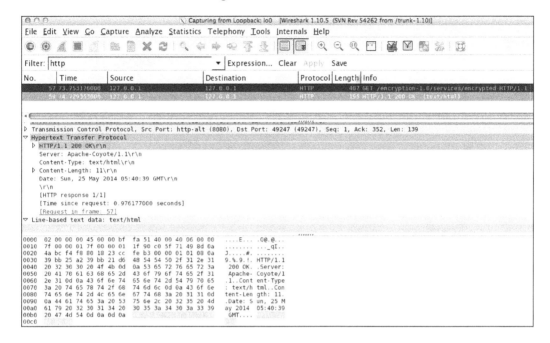

As we can see, the traffic analyzer shows how all the information is traveling straight and how easily it is interpreted. Now, let's enable HTTPS on JBoss to show how the whole message is encrypted.

Enabling the server with HTTPS

So, first we have to create a certificate KeyStore. We can achieve this by executing the following command on the terminal:

```
keytool -genkey -alias tomcat -keyalg RSA
```

When it asks you for a password, you should use `changeit` as we have already used it in this book.

Now, we look at the `JBOSS_HOME/standalone/configuration/standalone.xml` file, at the line containing `<connector name="http"`, and add the following:

```
<connector name="https" protocol="HTTP/1.1" scheme="https"
socket-binding="https" secure="true">
  <ssl/>
</connector>
```

Once you've made this change, we will restart the application server, deploy the application, and edit the request. This time, we'll use port 8443 and the HTTPS protocol. So, the URL should look like the following:

```
https://localhost:8443/encryption-1.0/services/encrypted
```

Let's execute the request using SoapUI; our traffic analyzer will now show us the following result:

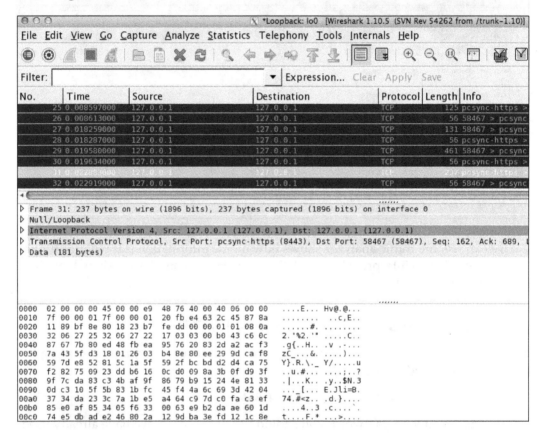

As we expected, this time, the analyzer shows us very clearly that all the information has been encrypted.

Moving forward with our example, we will now disable HTTPS in JBoss. For this, we have to remove the connector we added before. Now, we will use S/MIME in order to encrypt only the message body of the response. First, let's check some concepts that will help us understand how it works.

S/MIME comes from Secure MIME. MIME stands for Multipurpose Internet Mail Extension, which helps us to not only send messages such as "Hello world", but also to send more interesting content such as videos, audio, and so on. MIME works with e-mail protocols such as SMTP and HTTP. This helps us to work with RESTful S/MIME web services. On the other hand, MIME offers us the following features:

- Message encryption
- Validating the identity of the user who sends the message
- The capability to verify the information integrity of the message

Given that S/MIME works with certifications, this is where the information of the message sender is saved. When the receiver gets the message, they observe all the public part of the message. The message can then be deciphered using a key. Also, the receiver can access its content. If you want to proceed further with S/MIME, we recommend you visit the link `http://datatracker.ietf.org/wg/smime/charter/`.

Let's start by making some changes. First, we will create the source folder `src/main/resources` in the application; in this directory, we will place the resources necessary to encrypt the message.

Then, we generate a certificate using `openssl`, go to the directory we just created from the console, and run the following at the command line on a terminal:

```
openssl req -x509 -nodes -days 365 -newkey rsa:1024 -keyout demokey.pem
-out democert.pem
```

Now, we have to enter the requested information as shown in the following screenshot:

This will generate two files: demokey.pem, which is a private key, and democert.pem, which is a certificate we will use to encrypt the message body. To represent a signed response, RESTEasy uses the EnvelopedOutput object. In the following figure, we show you how RESTEasy encrypts messages:

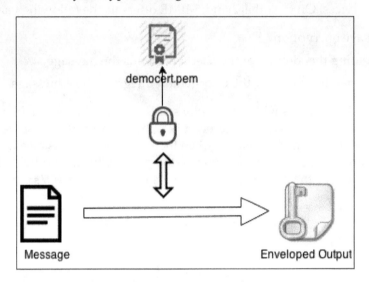

Therefore, we must replace the return type of the method gretting() in the EncryptedService class. Let's change the string to EnvelopedOutput and encrypt the message body using the certificate we generated before. Applying these changes, our method should look like the following:

```
@GET
public EnvelopedOutput gretting() throws Exception {
  InputStream certPem = Thread.currentThread()
                      .getContextClassLoader()
                      .getResourceAsStream("democert.pem");
  X509Certificate myX509Certificate = PemUtils.
      decodeCertificate(certPem)
  EnvelopedOutput output = new
    EnvelopedOutput("Hello world", MediaType.TEXT_PLAIN);
  output.setCertificate(myX509Certificate);
  return output;
}
```

Let's make a change in the `pom.xml` file. We will modify the `dependencies` section in the following way:

```
<dependencies>
  <dependency>
    <groupId>junit</groupId>
    <artifactId>junit</artifactId>
    <version>4.8.1</version>
  </dependency>
  <dependency>
    <groupId>org.jboss.resteasy</groupId>
    <artifactId>resteasy-jaxrs</artifactId>
    <version>3.0.6.Final</version>
    <scope>provided</scope>
  </dependency>
  <dependency>
    <groupId>org.jboss.resteasy</groupId>
    <artifactId>resteasy-jaxb-provider</artifactId>
    <version>3.0.6.Final</version>
    <scope>provided</scope>
  </dependency>
  <dependency>
    <groupId>org.jboss.resteasy</groupId>
    <artifactId>resteasy-crypto</artifactId>
    <version>3.0.6.Final</version>
  </dependency>
</dependencies>
```

Notice how we changed the scope of the `resteasy-jaxrs` and `resteasy-jaxb-provider` artifacts; this is necessary to avoid duplicate classes when we encrypt the message. Since these artifacts are modules within the application server, you need to indicate that we want to load them. For this, we will modify the `pom.xml` file in the plugin section of `maven-war-plugin`, as follows:

```
<plugin>
  <groupId>org.apache.maven.plugins</groupId>
  <artifactId>maven-war-plugin</artifactId>
  <configuration>
    <failOnMissingWebXml>false</failOnMissingWebXml>
    <archive>
      <manifestEntries>
        <Dependencies>org.jboss.resteasy.resteasy-jaxb-provider
          export, org.jboss.resteasy.resteasy-jaxrs
          export</Dependencies>
      </manifestEntries>
```

```
      </archive>
    </configuration>
  </plugin>
```

Since JBoss Version 7 is a module-based application server, by default, only a few modules are activated when it starts. If you want to access other modules, it is necessary to indicate these dependencies explicitly. This can be done through the `MANIFEST.MF` file or by creating a file called `jboss-deployment-structure.xml`.

In this case, we will choose the first file by using `maven-war`-plugin to indicate the required dependencies.

Testing the functionality

Now, let's make the request again from SoapUI to the URL `http://localhost:8080/encryption-1.0/services/encrypted`.

This time, the response we will get is shown in the following screenshot:

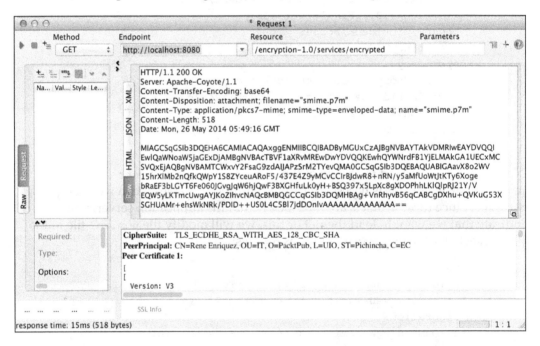

The following is what we will see from the traffic analyzer:

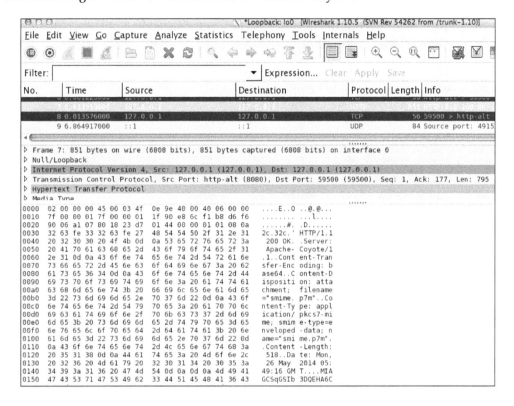

As we can see, it shows us something very similar to the response from SoapUI. To decrypt the content, it is necessary that we have the private key and certificate. Through these two resources, we can obtain the object `EnvelopedInput` and get the message from it, as shown in the following figure:

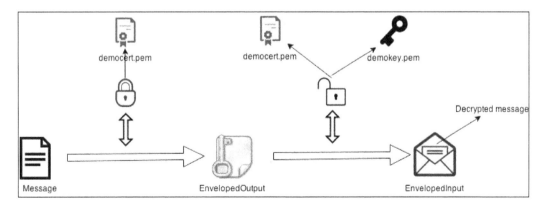

This will be demonstrated in the following code through a unit test. However, before going forward, we want to show that when encrypting messages with S/MIME, headers remain readable but the message body is fully encrypted. So, if we do not have the resources, the information is outdated and cannot be interpreted.

Now, we will write a class that allows us to read the message body. For this, we will create a new source folder called `src/main/test`.

Within this folder, let's create the class `com.packtpub.EncryptedServiceTest` with the following content:

```
package com.packtpub;

import java.security.PrivateKey;
import java.security.cert.X509Certificate;

import javax.ws.rs.client.Client;
import javax.ws.rs.client.WebTarget;

import junit.framework.Assert;

import org.jboss.resteasy.client.jaxrs.ResteasyClientBuilder;
import org.jboss.resteasy.security.PemUtils;
import org.jboss.resteasy.security.smime.EnvelopedInput;
import org.junit.Test;

public class EncryptedServiceTest {

  @Test
  public void testEncryptedGet() throws Exception {
    // LOADING THE CERTIFICATE
    X509Certificate myX509Certificate =
      PemUtils.decodeCertificate(
        Thread
        .currentThread().getContextClassLoader()
        .getResourceAsStream("democert.pem"));
    // LOADING THE KEY
    PrivateKey myPrivateKey = PemUtils.decodePrivateKey(Thread
        .currentThread().getContextClassLoader()
        .getResourceAsStream("demokey.pem"));
    // CREATING A CLIENT FOR THE WEB SERVICE
    Client client = new ResteasyClientBuilder().build();
    WebTarget target = client.target(
      "http://localhost:8080/encryption-1.0/services/encrypted"
    );
```

```
// RETRIEVING THE RESULT OF METHOD EXECUTION
EnvelopedInput<?> input = target.request().
        get(EnvelopedInput.class);
Assert.assertEquals("Hello world",
    input.getEntity(String.class,
    myPrivateKey, myX509Certificate));
client.close();
    }

}
```

Note how we need both the private key and the certificate to decrypt the message to obtain the entity formed from a string containing the message `Hello world`.

When we run this unit test, we should get a green bar if all goes well. This indicates that to decrypt the message, using the previous resources (private key and certificate) has obtained the expected message.

Summary

In this chapter, we worked with digital signatures and learned how to use them in RESTful web services. These days, digital signatures are often used because they guarantee message integrity, and information cannot be compromised while it is traveling from the sender to the receptor. We already know that information can be modified in transit, but when you're verifying the signed information, the receiver can notice it and take the actions that he/she believes are appropriate. For example, they can send another request to avoid working with corrupt information. At the end of this chapter, we worked with message body encryption, and we saw the difference between using these encryptions and HTTPS. Finally, we saw how the receiver, using the key, figured out the message body to make use of the information according to their needs.

Index

SSO
  about 77
  configuring, for security
    management 77, 78

T

TLS
  features 25, 26
**tools, for RESTful web services
    environment setup**
  Apache Maven 3.1.1 8
  Eclipse IDE 8
  JBoss AS 7.1.1 Final 8

JDK 1.7.x 8
SoapUI 4.6 8
Transport layer security. *See* **TLS**

V

version property 9

W

Wireshark
  columns 31
  URL 26

Thank you for buying
RESTful Java Web Services Security

About Packt Publishing

Packt, pronounced 'packed', published its first book "*Mastering phpMyAdmin for Effective MySQL Management*" in April 2004 and subsequently continued to specialize in publishing highly focused books on specific technologies and solutions.

Our books and publications share the experiences of your fellow IT professionals in adapting and customizing today's systems, applications, and frameworks. Our solution based books give you the knowledge and power to customize the software and technologies you're using to get the job done. Packt books are more specific and less general than the IT books you have seen in the past. Our unique business model allows us to bring you more focused information, giving you more of what you need to know, and less of what you don't.

Packt is a modern, yet unique publishing company, which focuses on producing quality, cutting-edge books for communities of developers, administrators, and newbies alike. For more information, please visit our website: www.packtpub.com.

About Packt Open Source

In 2010, Packt launched two new brands, Packt Open Source and Packt Enterprise, in order to continue its focus on specialization. This book is part of the Packt Open Source brand, home to books published on software built around Open Source licenses, and offering information to anybody from advanced developers to budding web designers. The Open Source brand also runs Packt's Open Source Royalty Scheme, by which Packt gives a royalty to each Open Source project about whose software a book is sold.

Writing for Packt

We welcome all inquiries from people who are interested in authoring. Book proposals should be sent to author@packtpub.com. If your book idea is still at an early stage and you would like to discuss it first before writing a formal book proposal, contact us; one of our commissioning editors will get in touch with you.

We're not just looking for published authors; if you have strong technical skills but no writing experience, our experienced editors can help you develop a writing career, or simply get some additional reward for your expertise.

open source*
community experience distilled

RESTful Web Services
with Dropwizard

Over 20 recipes to help you build high-performance,
production-ready RESTful JVM-based backend services

Alexandros Dallas

RESTful Web Services with Dropwizard

ISBN: 978-1-78328-953-0   Paperback: 112 pages

Over 20 recipes to help you build high-performance,
production-ready RESTful JVM-based backend
services

1. Learn how to build and test your own
   high-performance web service application.

2. Know more about creating and serving custom
   database content with web services.

3. Gain insight on how to secure your
   web service.

Developing RESTful Web
Services with Jersey 2.0

Create RESTful web services smoothly using the robust
Jersey 2.0 and JAX-RS APIs

Sunil Gulabani

Developing RESTful Web Services with Jersey 2.0

ISBN: 978-1-78328-829-8   Paperback: 98 pages

Create RESTful web services smoothly using the
robust Jersey 2.0 and JAX-RS APIs

1. Understand and implement the Jersey and
   JAX-RS APIs with ease.

2. Construct top-notch server- and client-side
   web services.

3. Learn about server-sent events, for showing
   real-time data.

Please check **www.PacktPub.com** for information on our titles

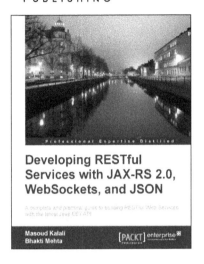

Developing RESTful
Services with JAX-RS 2.0,
WebSockets, and JSON

Masoud Kalali
Bhakti Mehta

[PACKT] enterprise

Developing RESTful Services with JAX-RS 2.0, WebSockets, and JSON

ISBN: 978-1-78217-812-5   Paperback: 128 pages

A complete and practical guide to building RESTful Web Services with the latest Java EE7 API

1. Learning about different client/server communication models including but not limited to client polling, server-sent events, and WebSockets.

2. Efficiently use WebSockets, server-sent events, and JSON in Java EE applications.

3. Learn about JAX-RS 2.0 new features and enhancements.

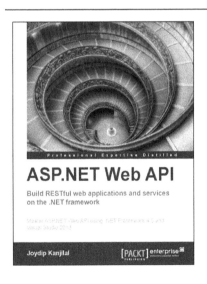

ASP.NET Web API

Build RESTful web applications and services on the .NET framework

Joydip Kanjilal

[PACKT] enterprise

ASP.NET Web API

Build RESTful web applications and services on the .NET framework

ISBN: 978-1-84968-974-8   Paperback: 224 pages

Master ASP.NET Web API using .NET Framework 4.5 and Visual Studio 2013

1. Clear and concise guide to the ASP.NET Web API with plentiful code examples.

2. Learn about the advanced concepts of the WCF-windows communication foundation.

3. Explore ways to consume Web API services using ASP.NET, ASP.NET MVC, WPF, and Silverlight clients.

Please check **www.PacktPub.com** for information on our titles

www.ingramcontent.com/pod-product-compliance
Lightning Source LLC
Chambersburg PA
CBHW060148060326
40690CB00018B/4034